MW01291683

POWERLESS?

Unveiling the Truth
About Addiction Recovery

Introducing an Empowering
New 21st-Century Approach

Richard H. & Dawn M. Johnson

Spring 2020 Edition
Copyright © 2018 Richard H. & Dawn M. Johnson

Published by Kerith Resources
Kerithresources.com

ABOUT THE COVER

You will notice the outlets and plug on the cover do not look like the ones found in the United States. Unless you have traveled in Europe, they may appear strange to you.

Until you get used to them.

We are used to traditional recovery. Since the 1930s, its slogans and tenets have become ingrained in our psyche and culture. It is "the way we have always done things."

The problem is, traditional recovery programs based on the twelve steps are not working. Only 5-10% of addicts who seek help successfully recover.

A new century calls for a new approach. It may seem strange at first until it starts to work for you. Change is not always comfortable.

Until you get used to it.

We begin with something traditional recovery programs will likely never tell you:

YOU ARE NOT POWERLESS!

Cover Concept and Design:
Suzanna L. Jacobson

A NOTE FROM THE AUTHORS

We did not write this book for academics or scholars, who may not be satisfied with our informal language style or the limited number of footnotes.

We wrote it for the millions of people who wrestle with addictive behavior and its effects. We used simple, everyday language to make our book easy to read, and as empowering as possible.

Concerning Recovery Success Rates

Throughout the book, we reference a 5-10% success rate for traditional recovery programs based on the twelve steps. This success rate is an average derived from several sources. Here are a few of them:

> Report Title: *"Alcoholics Anonymous (AA) is a self-help group, organized through an international organization of recovering alcoholics, that offers emotional support and a model of abstinence for people recovering from alcohol dependence using a 12-step approach."* The Cochrane Foundation examined studies conducted over a forty-year period between 1966 and 2005. Published by the Cochrane Collaboration, July 19, 2006. (Cochrane.org)
>
> *"Why Heroin Relapse Rate is So High,"* by Caroline McGraw, Published January 14, 2017, by The Clearing. (theclearingnw.com).
>
> *"The Sober Truth"* by Lance Dodes, page 74: *"An objective calculation puts AA's success rate at 5-8%."*

DEDICATION

We dedicate this book to all who suffer;
not only addicts but also those who love them.

May you find what you need in these pages.

ACKNOWLEDGMENTS

We wish to thank our family and friends. They have walked along the road to freedom with us all these years, and both challenged and encouraged us.

We also thank the Father, Son, and Holy Spirit for the revelation, patience, and empowerment we needed to complete this book.

God's love, mercy, and friendship have given our lives meaning and purpose and birthed in us a desire to see everyone become permanently whole and free.

TABLE OF CONTENTS

TO BEGIN

This book is for addicts, whether actively using or in recovery and those who love them.

No one gets into trouble alone. No one recovers alone.

First, we will explore how we got into trouble. Then, we will discuss how to get out of it.

Our purpose is to help addicts and their families:

- ❖ Break the vicious downward spiral of addiction
- ❖ Attain successful recovery
- ❖ Become permanently whole and free

There is a difference between recovery and freedom. We will discuss that difference later.

The Family is Important

Addicts are not the only ones affected by addiction, but they seem to get most, if not all, the attention.

We want to change that.

To ensure the hurts and needs of family members are also acknowledged and addressed, our *My Recovery Community* offers help and hope for addicts and family members alike.

If you are an addict who wants to stop using, you will need help to do it. No doubt, you already know that.

If one of your family members is an addict, you will need help, too, whether they stop using or not.

You may need as much help and healing as you believe your addicted family member does, and possibly more.

Your recovery is just as important as theirs.

Addicts are laser-focused on using. Using is the most important thing to them.

They are generally not mindful of the damage their behavior does to those who love them.

They may not remember what they said or did while under the influence. If an addict does remember, their recollection is likely to be foggy or self-serving.

Addicts may isolate themselves from their families, or their families may break off contact with them.

No matter who initiates it, breaking off contact will not prevent an addict's behavior from continuing to hurt and harm those who love them.

Being in recovery can be like peeling an onion. We will cry as we remove each layer.

It may take time to get past the disappointment, anger, and frustration in the top layers, and begin to deal with the hidden trauma and painful emotions hiding below.

But the family that peels together heals together!

Freedom is Possible

Recovery is good, but it is not complete. Freedom is complete.

Recovery is not the destination, as many believe, but part of a personal journey to wholeness.

Living in recovery does not mean we must live in recovery for the rest of our lives. Complete freedom is possible.

Why settle for crumbs from life's table, when we can have a seat at the banquet and eat until we are full?

Why live in fear of relapse, when we can become whole and live without fear?

The Root of Addictive Behavior

Society has been trying to solve our alcoholism and other addiction issues for generations. We have seen significant progress in recent years, but the root cause of addictive behavior has eluded us.

Until now.

The root cause of addictive behavior is a sense or spirit of powerlessness.

Entirely unaddressed by traditional recovery programs, this sense of powerlessness has become a pervasive and destructive force in millions of lives.

Whether we are truly powerless, or only believe we are, the result is the same - emotional pain.

Our most common response to pain - self-medicate to numb or avoid it.

Addicts are not the only ones who struggle with a sense or spirit of powerlessness. Family, friends, co-workers, and children do, too.

Not knowing what to do, they must witness the agonizing self-destruction of someone they love.

Addicts suffer the consequences of their addiction. Those who love them suffer, as well.

Obsessing about a loved one's addictive behavior and need for healing can distract us from our own need for healing.

We want to do something, but we may not know what to do or where to turn for help.

Without our being aware of its existence and influence, a sense of powerlessness takes root and grows as time passes, and things grow worse.

The spirit of powerlessness lies at the bottom of our emotional well, driving a host of distressful emotions and setting the stage for addiction to take over our lives.

A Matter of the Heart: Changing our behavior is an excellent first step toward recovery and freedom, but the ultimate solution for addiction is to facilitate a <u>change of heart</u>.

Our goal is not "white-knuckled sobriety" nor a lifetime "in recovery." Our goal is complete and permanent freedom from addiction and its causes.

Freedom is possible if you want it. It is your choice to make.

What do you want to do?

Maintaining Our Focus

Tempting as it may be to follow relevant but distracting rabbit trails, we want to stay focused on our primary purpose; to help addicts and families break the vicious downward spiral of addiction, achieve successful recovery, and become whole.

We will touch on several topics along the way related to addiction, recovery, and freedom that deserve books of their own.

You may believe you are alone, but you are not alone.

Fellow travelers who care about and want to help surround you.

The *My Recovery Community,* based on this book, offers a new approach to addiction recovery for addicts and families alike.

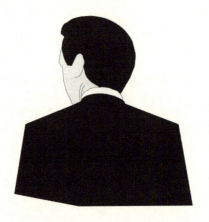

No matter what form addictive
behavior may take, the root
cause driving it is the same - a
sense or spirit of powerlessness.

"HOUSTON, WE HAVE A PROBLEM."

We are in trouble.

Today's explosion of addictive behavior, the low success rates of traditional twelve-step recovery programs, and the collateral damage suffered by addicts' families and society require a new approach to addiction recovery.

Twelve Step Recovery Doesn't Work

Many people are surprised to learn recovery programs based on the twelve steps do not work for most of those who turn to them for help.

How do we know they don't work? Because today's addiction recovery rates are unacceptably low:

- ❖ Only one in ten (10%) of the approximately twenty-five million addicts in the United States aged twelve and older seeks help to stop using.

- ❖ Of the one in ten addicts who seek help to stop, only one in ten (5-10%) recovers.

In short, only one addict in one hundred (1%) successfully stops using.

Why don't traditional recovery programs work? Because they deal with the symptoms rather than the root cause of addiction.

For the same reason, expensive rehabs don't work, either.

"Wait a minute...twelve-step recovery is working for me!"

That's great! We're very happy for you and anyone else who successfully recovers, no matter how they do it.

If you are one of the few people for whom traditional addiction recovery is working, then keep doing what you're doing.

We're concerned about the 90-95% who fall by the wayside.

We want them to succeed, too.

One is the Loneliest Number

We're at a typical recovery group meeting. There are one hundred people there, talking, drinking coffee, and waiting for the meeting to start:

- ❖ Fifty have been sober and clean for less than three months

- ❖ Thirty-six have been sober and clean for three months

- ❖ Eleven have been sober and clean for two years

- ❖ Three have been sober and clean for twenty years or longer

Of the three people with more than twenty years' sobriety, only one will enjoy life-long sobriety without relapse.

What is the Source of the 5-10% Recovery Rate?

The 5-10% success rate figure comes from a survey of forty years' worth of studies. These studies used control groups and were peer-reviewed.[1]

The survey did not include studies lacking control groups or those designed to yield pre-determined desired results.

Study participants assigned to a control group received no help for their addictions, while those in a second group received some form of assistance.

Control group recovery rates ranged from 5 to 8%.

Control group participants received no help at all, yet almost as many recovered without help as recovered with help!

This phenomenon is called "spontaneous recovery." It means some addicts simply stop using for no apparent reason. [2]

Up to 8% of control group members did nothing and recovered, while up to 10% of the group that did something recovered.

With only two percentage points separating the control group from the other group, these studies seem to suggest doing nothing is almost as effective as doing something.

If you owned a company whose service only worked 5-10% of the time, how long do you think you could stay in business?

---

[1] See "*A Note from the Authors*" at the beginning of this book.
[2] "*Spontaneous Recovery in Alcoholics: A Review and Analysis of the Available Research*" by R. G. Smart. Drug and Alcohol Dependence 1(1975-76): 284.

Yet we've been doing addiction recovery the same way for more than eighty years.

We keep on with it, even though it does not work for most of the people who seek help.

It's long past time to do something different.

Why are Recovery Rates So Low?

Meeting Attendance is a Sentencing Option: Decades ago, judges began to order defendants convicted of substance abuse-related offenses to attend recovery group meetings, whether they wanted to recover or not.

As mandatory meeting attendance became a widely-accepted sentencing option, an increasing number of people came to meetings, not because they wanted to stop drinking or using drugs, but to stay out of prison.

They came to get their paperwork signed, to prove they had complied with the terms of their probation or parole.

Perhaps they stayed for the whole meeting. Perhaps they even listened. If we can judge by the 5-10% recovery rate, most continued to use.

An organization may be able to absorb a few people who do not share their vision and values or subscribe to their purpose.

However, a large-scale influx of "members" indifferent or hostile to their cause will dilute their culture and cripple their mission.

This is what has happened to AA.

Meetings Attract Drug Dealers: Former drug dealers tell us recovery meetings, halfway houses, and token clubs are prime places to sell drugs.

It's like the Girl Scouts setting up a table outside a marijuana store to sell cookies. It's smart marketing.

If some people going to meetings intend to keep using drugs, then someone will likely be there to sell them.

When newcomers attend their first meeting, they may encounter predators waiting to take advantage of their vulnerability. Temptation plus availability often equals relapse.

The Root Cause of Addiction is Not Addressed: The peer support found in traditional recovery programs is one of its strengths.

It can help people stop their addictive behavior, though, for most, sobriety is only maintained for a few months or years.

As helpful and powerful as peer support can be, twelve-step recovery fails because it does not address the sense or spirit of powerlessness at the root of addictive behavior.

Forty years' worth of low recovery rates indicates they are in the dark concerning addiction's root emotional cause.

If they knew what it was, they would, no doubt, have addressed it by now, and today's recovery rates would be higher.

Richard: Before we continue, you should know Alcoholics Anonymous got me started on the road to recovery. '

While it ultimately does not work for most people, it worked well enough to help me stop drinking and using drugs until the emotional root cause of my addictive behavior came to the surface. Then it was addressed.

I will always be thankful for the love, encouragement, support, and much-needed doses of reality they gave me. AA kept me alive.

Twelve-step recovery may not work for most people, but it does work for some.

For a very long time, AA was the only option for alcoholics seeking help. Millions of people have successfully stopped drinking thanks to "The Program."

If AA or any other recovery program is working for you, keep going. You may very well be that one person in one hundred who makes it. We just need something else for the ninety-nine people who fall by the wayside.

If the Media Upped Their Game

Given the media's extensive coverage of addiction's destructive power, one might reasonably expect to see at least occasional reports on addiction recovery's universally low success rates.

We would be better-informed concerning what works and what doesn't. We could stop funding poorly-performing programs and invest the savings in new ways to break addiction's power.

But - recovery success rates are not widely reported.

When the media does a story on a recovery program, they usually present only anecdotal evidence (the personal stories of individual recovering addicts) as proof of success.

We are very happy for every person who recovers. We enjoy hearing their success stories, but to win the war against addiction, we need more than stories of individual success.

We need valid data showing actual success rates.

Without reliable information tested and authenticated by unbiased researchers, we cannot make informed decisions concerning where to invest our resources - or send someone for help.

The media boasts about "speaking truth to power" and holding people accountable; perhaps they should look in the mirror.

Their coverage of addiction and recovery is too often shallow and breathlessly over-dramatized.

In their rush to publish, the media doesn't always double-check the information they receive. They sometimes rely too much on "authoritative sources" with a financial stake in the outcome.

Their coverage frequently falls short of traditional standards of quality journalism. They are not asking the right questions.

Before they tout the success of any recovery program, the media should stop relying only on people's stories to prove it, no matter how inspiring those stories may be.

They ought to get specific answers to these questions:

1. What is your success rate?

2. How do you define success?

3. What percentage of your program participants drop out without completing it?

4. When you determine your success rate, do you factor in participants who drop out?

5. Why do participants drop out?

6. How do you follow up on participants, and for how long after they leave or complete your program, to get the data you need to determine your success rate?

Inspiration is not enough. We need reliable information, too.

Rehabs: Costly and Ineffective

These are also excellent questions to ask of rehabs and any other program before you give them your money. Most will not be able to provide you with straight-forward answers.

Assessing a program's success rate with any accuracy is not possible without knowing how many people drop out without completing it.

We cannot determine a rehab program's success rate unless we know what number and percentage of people drop out, and why.

Without counting drop-outs, it becomes possible to have a 100% success rate if 99 of 100 people drop out of a program, and only one person completes it and stops using!

Rehabs will gladly take your money; as much as $30-100,000 for a month's worth of residential "treatment" in some cases.

Don't give it to them.

We have met too many family members who emptied their savings accounts, dug into their retirement funds, mortgaged their homes and ran up an enormous debt, to send a loved one to rehab - only to see them relapse after they returned home.

Many addicts tell us they think rehabs are a joke. They said the "help" they received was worthless, or no different from the help they could have gotten free of charge by attending a recovery group meeting in a church basement.

At some rehabs, the supervision was so lax, that residents could leave the premises, buy whatever they wanted, and return without detection.

Some have been to a dozen or more rehabs and continue to use. Most have lost hope they will ever be able to stop.

FAMILY, FRIENDS, AND OUTCOMES

Addicts' family members often need the same change of heart, and emotional healing as addicts do for a straightforward reason; they have become trapped in a dysfunctional emotional cycle.

The Cycle of Dysfunction

The cycle of dysfunction is a downward spiral. It's a dance that the addicts and their families dance together.

The cycle can range from mildly unbalanced to dangerously life-threatening in intensity.

Physical violence may also be possible.

The cycle's destructive effects grow worse over time. Without intervention, it will continue until it wears everyone out.

Or someone dies. It can be that serious.

People remain in the cycle because they do not know any other way to relate to other people.

None of their relationships are healthy.

Intimate Partnerships: People entrenched in the cycle tend to be attracted to other people trapped in the cycle.

Their mutual dysfunction guarantees their relationships with "significant others" will be unhealthy, and possibly toxic.

For people in the cycle, their relationships seem healthy and normal. They do not grasp how unhealthy and potentially dangerous their relationships may be.

For example, many assume all married couples fight - but this is not true. Partners in a healthy marriage may not always agree, but they know how to communicate and compromise.

They work out their differences without saying or doing things they will later regret. They have learned the art of being honest about how they feel and are good at listening to one another.

Love-Based Relationships: When there is conflict in a love-based relationship, the partners' shared goal is to re-establish and maintain intimacy.

There is no winner and no loser. They win together and lose together.

When they are angry at one another, they do not allow it to linger until it becomes bitterness. Instead, the partners admit, express, and deal with it as quickly and honestly as they can.

They do not allow minor annoyances to become significant issues.

Both partners are powerful and share their power. They do not desire to gain control at their partner's expense.

Power-Based Relationships: When there is conflict in a power-based relationship, the goal of each partner is to win.

In their conflicts, there will be a winner and a loser.
They compensate for their sense of powerlessness by trying to control the other partner.

The partner who wins consistently will continue to push for more power. As they continue to lose ground, the losing partner's resentment will become lingering anger.

Outbursts triggered by relatively minor irritants will become more frequent as the losing partner tries to retain or regain power.

Neither partner knows what love is. They confuse love with having their needs and desires satisfied.

They don't know a spirit of powerlessness is driving the power struggle in their relationship. They are unaware their liaison is unhealthy.

Manipulation

People in unhealthy relationships often dominate their partners through manipulation. They will do whatever it takes to get the other person to do what they want.

As one partner gains power over the other, it becomes more difficult for the submissive partner to resist.

In extreme cases, the submissive partner may come to doubt the evidence of their senses and mistrust their judgment.

They hand over their decision-making power to the dominant partner and may eventually become incapable of independent thought or action.[3]

Addicts are not the only ones who manipulate others to get what they want. Those who love them, who may feel pressured by an addict's demands, may also resort to manipulation to regain their power.

Family members frustrated by endless broken promises may use manipulative tactics to force their addicted family member to stop using and get help.

These are some of the tools people use to manipulate others:

- ❖ Guilt
- ❖ Withholding ("You can't have _____ until you _____.")
- ❖ Bribery ("I will give you _____ if you will _____.")
- ❖ Ignoring/dismissing the other person's thoughts or feelings
- ❖ Nagging
- ❖ Shaming or embarrassing the other person
- ❖ Ridicule

Emotionally healthy people don't manipulate. They simply ask for what they want.

_____

[3] This is called "gaslighting," after the movie *Gaslight* starring Ingrid Bergman and Charles Boyer.

Breaking versus Perpetuating the Cycle

Whether the addict in your family is in recovery or still using your relationship with them is likely to be emotionally unhealthy. It could become toxic.

The dysfunction may have begun before addiction took hold. It may also be a by-product of addictive behavior.

No matter how it started, and wherever it may fall on the intensity scale, recognizing you are involved in a dysfunctional relationship is an essential step toward your recovery.

We can break the cycle of dysfunction. Unfortunately, too many people break out of it in an unhealthy way.

The most common unhealthy exit occurs when someone ends the relationship without dealing with the issues that lead them into toxic relationships in the first place. They then begin another dysfunctional relationship with someone else.

A new cycle is born.

Until they become whole, addicts will always look for another enabler, and enablers will invariably find someone to enable.

Emotionally unhealthy people are attracted to other emotionally unhealthy people. Emotionally healthy people are attracted to other emotionally healthy people.

An emotionally stable person may become a friend, but they will not be interested in forming an intimate relationship with an addict or an enabler.

In their interactions with people in the cycle, emotionally healthy people will not allow themselves to become entangled in the drama. They will maintain their integrity and emotional health.

They will confront and reject attempts to manipulate them and will retain the power to say "no."

The healthy and best way to break the cycle of dysfunction is to swallow our pride and get help.

Other people can show us what healthy relationships look like, help us recognize where we need to change, give us tools to facilitate positive change, and offer suggestions and support to help us improve.

Please don't let pride or fear rob you of a chance for peace and freedom.

"It's All Their Fault!"

Family members tend to believe their addicted family member is the problem. They hope life will return to normal; that everything will be fine after they stop using. It is not often so.

With most of their attention focused on trying to fix an addict, family members often neglect their own need for help.

Until they understand they need at least as much healing as addicts do, they will not seek help for themselves.

> Dawn: My father has a saying: "The last family member to receive their healing will be the most miserable."

When family members find healing and take back their power, addicts' attempts to manipulate them stop working. They no longer produce the desired results.

Whether an addict or a family member, we reach a critical point after we lose our power to manipulate others. We have a choice to make.

We can escalate our attempts to manipulate others, a course of action unlikely to work, or we can concede that the game is over, acknowledge our need for healing, and begin a journey to recovery and freedom.

Family relationships may have been mildly dysfunctional before addiction became an issue.

If so, you can still get help to avoid the escalation of dysfunction that leads to addictive behavior.

If your family relationships are already severely dysfunctional, don't wait. Get help right away before someone gets hurt.

Broken Connectors

An inability to connect with other people is a common problem for powerless people caught up in addictive behavior. It can lead to chronic loneliness, isolation, and a pervasive sense of being an outcast or outsider.

Some people become loners even though many around them love and cherish them.

They have broken love-connectors; they cannot recognize, receive, or reciprocate love.

We are supposed to live in family and community, rather than in isolation.

We need companionship and love. We need to belong. Living as an outcast is damaging to the soul.

Frequent recovery group meeting attendance can help break the power of loneliness and repair our broken connectors.

Going to a meeting every day is even better, especially for people new to recovery.

Richard: That's what happened to me near the end of my first year in AA.

I was sitting in a meeting listening to the discussion when I suddenly realized I was no longer lonely!

I could not point to the moment my loneliness disappeared, but that didn't matter. I was simply happy to rejoin humanity.

It was a powerful healing moment.

Procrastination

Procrastinators never take "now" for an answer.

Procrastinators hope relationship issues and other problems will go away if they ignore them. They may also fail to act out of fear of offending someone.

Doing nothing seems to be the best course. It isn't.

Failure to deal with issues promptly may eventually lead to more significant problems. Time digs a deeper hole out of which we must climb.

It is always best to deal with issues while they are still relatively small before they get out of hand.

Addictive behavior always becomes worse over time if it remains unchecked.

The longer it goes on, the harder it will be for both addicts and family members to recover.

Confrontation

Most people hate confrontation and try to avoid it, but some people relish and deliberately provoke it. These folks tend to be control freaks, enslaved by a hidden spirit of powerlessness.

Confrontation is part of their game. To empower themselves, addicts drain power from others. To get their way, they will bully, manipulate, order everyone around, and demand obedience.

A child who grows up in a home where a controlling adult calls all the shots will not learn how to make wise decisions. To learn, children need opportunities to exercise the power of choice.

They become subject to a spirit of powerlessness and are at risk of engaging in addictive behavior.

Losing our power of choice is damaging. The forced surrender of our will to someone else is unnatural, dehumanizing, and painful. That's why we self-medicate to numb or avoid our pain.

Seek Your Healing: We cannot emphasize this enough; unless you want the one you love to fall deeper into addiction until they die, seek healing for yourself.

Your addicted family member's recovery deserves your attention. Just do not let their need consume you. Your well-being is just as important as theirs.

You cannot fix an addict or make their decisions for them, but you can decide to take care of yourself.

No matter what your addicted family member decides to do, persevere in your journey to wholeness.

A New Balance of Power

When addicts stop using and become contributing family members, other family members may not be as happy with the new reality as they had hoped to be.

People may have to give up some of their power to make room for recovering addicts to assume their share of family power and responsibilities.

A change in the balance of power within the family may make people uncomfortable.

The dance has changed. In extreme cases, another family member may take on the addict's role so that the dance may continue as before.

That's why it is best when the whole family recovers together.

Getting everyone on the same page is an important reason why family recovery is essential.

One woman described it this way:

"When my husband stopped drinking, he was in one recovery group, I was in another, and our children were in a third.

"These meetings helped, but what we really needed was to be in a group where we could be together and learn how to be a family again.

"No one seemed to know how to help us past the point of; 'He stopped drinking; now what do we do?'"

Possible Outcomes for Addicts

There are four possible outcomes for addicts:

Incarceration: People may go to prison for possessing, using, or selling illegal drugs.

Most incarcerated people (85%) are behind bars for substance abuse-related reasons. If we could solve our addiction problem, we could empty our prisons!

Hospitalization: The physical and emotional damage caused by abusing drugs or alcohol can ruin our health.

Hospitalization is more likely to occur as substance abuse takes a toll over time. If addicts avoid imprisonment, they may end up permanent residents of mental health or managed care facilities.

Death: Illegal drugs are not always as advertised. They are not often pure. They may contain additional harmful substances.

Substance abusers don't always know what they are buying.

Fentanyl, a highly dangerous drug, is sometimes mixed with heroin to give it an extra kick. Marijuana may also be treated with other substances to increase its potency.

Many addicts die by overdose. In their desire to "get a buzz," addicts use too much and die. If they avoid overdoing, addicts may die a slow death. A thirty-year-old may have the body and health issues of someone twice their age.

Substance abuse may not be the cause of death listed on the coroner's report, but it is usually a significant contributing factor.

Recovery: Sadly, this is the least frequent outcome.

Only 10% of addicts seek help to stop using. Of these, only 5-10% successfully recover. For the rest, the most likely outcome is hospitalization, prison, or death.

Possible Outcomes for Family Members

There are also four possible outcomes for family members of addicts.

One will occur, even if the addicted family member dies or is no longer in the picture:

Nothing Changes: Things are not likely to stay the same for long, though dysfunctional relationships sometimes last for years.

Dysfunctional relationships sometimes last because they are transactional relationships.

In a transactional relationship, people get something they value from the other person.

Addicts often groom enablers to give them drugs, money, food, shelter, sympathy, and whatever else they want.

Enablers get something in return; sympathy, a chance to play the martyr, and admiration for refusing to quit on someone they love.

Things Get Worse: Even if they lose hope for a good outcome, enablers soldier on, firmly entrenched in the idea they can fix or save an addict.

Enablers increasingly get their sense of self-worth from their rescue efforts. They won't give up. They have invested too much emotionally to quit.

The sympathy and attention they receive for their apparent self-sacrifice affirm them in their dysfunction. Martyrdom becomes an unhealthy part of their identity.

Break the Cycle in an Unhealthy Way: The cycle's downward spiral becomes so destructive that it ends the relationship, but not the dysfunction.

Unless addicts or enablers seek help to uncover and heal the emotional wounds that lead them into toxic relationships in the first place, they will start a new cycle in their next relationship.

Break the Cycle in a Healthy Way: This is the best and least common outcome.

When we choose a healthy way to break the cycle, it is because we have addressed the issues that set us up for dysfunction. We do not start a new cycle with anyone else.

We are well on our way to emotional wholeness. We will no longer respond to emotional blackmail, or allow anyone to draw us into a dysfunctional cycle of drama and chaos.

Their "crises" no longer become our emergencies. We may continue to help them, but no longer jump when they call.

We no longer lose ourselves in a futile effort to fix them.

Liberation!

"Your lack of planning and self-control does not constitute an emergency on my part."

These liberating words empower family members. They serve notice to addicts their manipulating days are over.

You may still choose to help an addict, but now it will be the kind of help they need, not the "help" they want.

If they reject your help and their life continues to get harder, an addict may blame you for it, and attempt to shame you into resuming the enablement of their self-destructive behavior.

Tell them you refuse to accept <u>any</u> responsibility for the results of their poor choices.

Remind them <u>they</u> decided to reject the help you offered.

Remind them that only <u>they</u> are responsible for their decisions and the consequences.
If your offer of real help still stands, tell them that, too.

After we learn the value and power of saying no to enablement, we stop wasting time, energy, and resources on people who do not want to change but only want to keep doing what they are doing.

And get us to pick up their tab.

We are then free if we so choose to help people who want to change.

Addicts who are serious about getting free will demonstrate they mean it with deeds, not words.

Ignore what addicts promise. Watch what they do.

Many people do not know there is such a thing as the cycle of dysfunction. If they know of it, they may be unwilling to admit their relationships fit the pattern.[4]

A lack of knowledge, not wanting to be embarrassed, and an unwillingness to embrace positive change, may keep people trapped in toxic relationships.

They may also be "comfortable" with the status quo. Fear of an unknown future may outweigh their present-day pain.

It doesn't have to be this way. Our hearts and lives can change.

We can become whole.

---

[4] It is more commonly known as the Cycle of Abuse. We didn't want to scare anyone.

You are <u>not</u> powerless!

MYTHS, TRUTHS, AND DEFINITIONS

Before we go further, let's dispel a few myths and define a few terms.

Since we're proposing a 21st-century approach to recovery, traditional definitions may not be as accurate as we need them to be.

We want people to understand what we mean by the terms we use clearly.

Addict Stereotypes

Many people picture someone with a needle in their arm, shooting heroin or some other "hard" drug. Or an unwashed, oily-haired drunk, stinking of alcohol and urine may come to mind.

Perhaps she lives on the streets, a cheap motel, or a homeless shelter. She carries her possessions in a shopping cart. She sells her body, panhandles, or shoplifts to pay for her next fix or bottle of cheap wine.

Most addicts do not fit these stereotypes at all. Addicts come in all shapes and sizes, from every economic and social class.

Addiction affects people living in inner-city neighborhoods, gated suburban communities, high-rise penthouses, and rural areas everywhere.

Addiction does not discriminate. Your affluent, well-educated neighbor may have a secret.

Tolerance/Tolerance Response

"Tolerance is the capacity of the body to endure or become less responsive to a substance such as a drug; especially with repeated use or exposure." [5]

The body adapts to the use of a physically-addictive substance and learns to tolerate its presence. Over time, it takes more substantial doses to produce the desired effect.

Addicts must increase the amount of the drug they use to attain the effect once achieved by a smaller dose. If they don't stop using, many addicts eventually overdose and die.

Not all drugs produce a physical tolerance response, but they can and often do produce an emotional dependency.

Addiction Defined

"The quality or state of being addicted."

This definition does not focus solely on substance abuse. It is broad enough to include other addictive behaviors such as sex, gambling, or shopping.

"A persistent, compulsive use of a substance known by the user to be harmful."

---

[5] Definitions in this chapter come from the *Merriam-Webster Dictionary* unless otherwise noted.

"A compulsive need for, and use of, a habit-forming substance, characterized by tolerance, and by well-defined physical symptoms upon withdrawal."

These definitions are also on target; however, there are a couple of things we ought to note about them.

Both focus solely on the abuse of substances. Addiction does not always involve the use of drugs or alcohol.

While a tolerance response can be a factor in <u>some</u> addictions, it is not always a factor.

It is certainly not a factor in addictive behaviors that do not involve the use of substances.

Joint Adventures

Marijuana (cannabis) is the most widely used and abused illegal drug in the United States.[6]

Its use does not produce a tolerance response, leading many marijuana smokers to believe it isn't harmful or addictive - a common belief among people who smoke the stuff.

They are right about not having a physical addiction, but they are wrong when they deny they may develop an emotional dependency on smoking weed.

Emotional dependency is still a dependency. Whether it is physical or psychological, addiction is a form of dependence.

Weed smokers often compare themselves to heroin addicts when they deny their emotional addiction to marijuana.

---

[6] National Institute on Drug Abuse

In their minds, heroin users are "the real addicts" because heroin is a physically-addictive "hard drug."

They rationalize smoking weed by claiming it's not nearly as bad as shooting heroin.

"Heroin kills people, but weed does not." So many marijuana smokers say, but the belief weed is harmless is not entirely correct:

It's Bad for the Brain: Research indicates smoking marijuana retards the development of the brain in young people. Children, teens, and young adults who smoke it may suffer damaging life-long consequences.[7]

It Causes Cancer: Smoking marijuana can cause various forms of cancer, just as tobacco does.

After decades of smoking weed (he didn't use tobacco in any form), one of our friends got cancer of the esophagus. It killed him.

Deaths on the Road: Every year, people are injured or killed by drivers under the influence of marijuana.

Advocates of legalization claim alcohol kills more people. They are right, but that still doesn't make marijuana harmless.

They rightly point out alcohol is legal, yet also kills. If drinking alcohol is legal, smokers claim, then smoking marijuana also ought to be legal

They fail to mention it is possible to drink alcohol <u>without getting drunk</u>.

---

[7] The Centers for Disease Control: cdc.gov

Millions of people around the world grab a beer while watching a sporting event, have a glass of wine with dinner, or enjoy a shot of whiskey to relax after a day's work, without becoming impaired.

People don't always drink alcohol to get drunk. You can't smoke marijuana without getting high.

Drunk drivers are a big enough problem. We should not add to the carnage by legalizing the sale and possession of pot.[8]

Given our self-indulgent culture, a society that has lost its way, and the potential billions of dollars to be made, we have no doubt the pro-legalization people will win.

No one can legitimately claim smoking marijuana doesn't harm or kill anyone. Lives don't matter to those who worship the almighty dollar.

Addiction Further Defined

Not all substances are physically addictive, yet their abuse is still an addiction. Addiction can involve the use of a substance, a behavior, or both.

For that reason, we have adopted the following definition:

"Addiction is a compulsive, frequently destructive behavior that dominates and controls our lives. It can manifest as:

❖ *Physical or emotional dependency on a substance that produces a tolerance response*

❖ *Emotional dependency on a substance that does not produce a tolerance response*

---

[8] In states where smoking marijuana has been legalized (Colorado, Vermont, and Massachusetts), usage has gone through the roof.

❖ *Emotional dependency on behavior that does not involve the use of any kind of substance."*

Addiction may also interfere with our ability to make responsible decisions, severely limit our range of options, makes it difficult or impossible to enjoy healthy relationships, and rob us of our power and freedom of choice.

Addiction Rebranded

Many medical and mental health professionals avoid the use of the word "addiction" to describe addiction. They prefer to use terms such as "substance-use disorder" or "alcohol-use disorder."

We do not choose to follow this trend for these reasons:

Addiction is a Behavior: We believe addiction is a behavior, not a disease.[9]

While the disease theory may have helped eliminate some of the stigma attached to addiction, and relieved at least some of the guilt and shame addicts may sometimes feel, too many addicts use it as an excuse to keep using.

---

[9] There are undoubtedly exceptions. Through substance-abuse, some people have caused damage to their brains and bodies that can be considered a chronic condition or disorder and will need to be treated as such.

Others may have been born with or acquired a mental or physical condition that makes them vulnerable to becoming an addict should they use.

Until they stop blaming a disease for their addictive behavior and accept personal responsibility for their decisions, most addicts will continue to use. Many will die.

Shock Value: Helping people get free and stay free frequently requires being ruthlessly honest and to the point.

Telling someone, "You have a disorder," doesn't have nearly the shock value of telling them, "You are an addict, and you're killing yourself." There's a time to be tactful, and a time to be blunt.

Language Matters

Dealing with addiction is a tough business. People often die.

Straight-forward language is sometimes necessary. Sometimes people die because no one confronted them with the unvarnished truth expressed in clear, no-nonsense terms.

To get the attention of active addicts, we must cut through the denial, excuses, outright lies, and the rest of the bull manure.

When someone is in imminent danger of death or severe injury, the best way to get their attention may be a verbal slap in the face.

In certain circumstances, confronting people with the hard truth, they have an addiction is much more to the point, and ultimately kinder, than telling them they have a substance-use disorder.

Pass the Blame, Please

"None of this is my fault. I have a disease."

Addicts are masters at passing the blame. It's a manipulation tactic and a survival skill.

When we call addictive behavior a disease or disorder, we hand addicts a convenient excuse to avoid taking responsibility for their choices.

Rather than take care of their own business, they will play the victim card to con others into giving them what they want. If we enable their self-destructive behavior, addicts will fail to stay sober and clean.

They are likely to die an early death by overdose, or to use the excuse countless inmates and addicts have been giving us for decades, by being "in the wrong place at the wrong time."

Recovery begins when addicts admit to themselves and others they have a problem and take personal responsibility for their lives, their decisions, and the consequences of their choices.

Pressuring addicts to take responsibility doesn't work. They must decide on their own to do it. Nothing good will happen until they do.

When helping someone take this first necessary step on their journey to wholeness, we try to be gentle when we can.

But sometimes only an unvarnished dose of reality, expressed in the bleakest, harshest terms, will do the job.

Rigorous honesty is necessary if we're going to help addicts stop using and get their lives and their power back. We will not let someone die because we were afraid to offend them.

Recovery Defined

Eighty-plus years of twelve-step recovery does not mean we understand what recovery is, what it looks like, or what it means to recover.

"Recovery is the act, process, or an instance of recovering; especially: an economic upturn (as after a depression)."

We like this statement. It provides us with a broad definition, using an economic upturn as an example. Who wouldn't want a full wallet after struggling to get by with an empty one?

"The process of combating a disorder (such as alcoholism), or a real or perceived problem."

This one works too, except for the reference to alcoholism as a disorder. Calling it a disorder can lead one to assume addictive behavior is a psychological or physiological disease.

Theories are Not Laws: The disease theory of addiction is not a scientific law. It is only a theory.

A theory is only a possible explanation for a phenomenon. It does not possess the weight or authority of scientific law.

With theories, there is always room for further research and revelation.

We do not believe addiction is a disease. That doesn't mean we're going to argue with people who think it is.

If believing it's a disease helps people recover, we're all for it.

Our issue is with those who use the disease theory to make billions of dollars off the misery of millions.

Modern-Day Snake Oil

Many residential rehab programs charge as much as $30-100k for a thirty-day stay.

Their accommodations and perks may be luxurious, but the "treatment" they offer is often nothing more than the same group meetings people can attend almost anywhere, free of charge.

Traditional recovery programs and rehabs produce the same dismal 5-10% success rate, but the church basement groups don't rob desperate people of their money and their hope.

Reaping excessive financial gain from promoting and offering recovery programs that do not work is just plain wrong.

Exploiting people in pain is evil.

Recovery is Normally a Process

While some people spontaneously recover (they simply and suddenly stop using), most recover over time.

A process is:

"A natural phenomenon marked by gradual changes that lead toward a particular result."

"A series of actions or operations leading to an end."

A process leads to an outcome.

The process itself is not an outcome, but a time-and-task line to help us achieve a goal, such as a journey to another city, the manufacture of a product, the delivery of a service, or becoming free of addiction.

Recovery is usually a series of gradual changes that help us achieve and maintain sobriety, though sudden, radical improvement may also occur.

What does it mean to recover? For most, it merely means to stop using.

People in recovery may have dealt with some of the emotional issues that contributed to their addictive behavior. They may also have tried to rebuild broken relationships.

The point is they're not using. That's progress!

Our destination is not recovery, though many people may be satisfied with living in recovery for the rest of their lives.

Our destination is freedom.

Freedom Defined

Freedom from addiction and recovery from addiction is not the same.

Recovery is a process that leads to freedom. Freedom is the destination.

Freedom is:

"The absence of necessity, coercion, or restraint in choice or action."

In the context of addiction, the absence of necessity, coercion, or constraint means we no longer have a reason or need to use. The barriers to freedom are gone.

That is one of the differences between recovery and freedom.

In recovery, the source of our pain generally remains but no longer drives us to self-medicate. We have learned how to live with or tolerate, our less than ideal emotional condition.

Most people who succeed in becoming sober and clean are content to remain "in recovery." They believe freedom is not possible.

But it is.

Recovery is better than using, but it is not complete. Freedom is complete.

Freedom is not the same as recovery. To be free means whatever motivated us to use, whether physical, emotional, or spiritual, is gone.

"The quality or state of being released, usually from something oppressive."

Without a doubt, addiction is oppressive. There is nothing good about becoming addicted.

Freedom is more than white-knuckled sobriety, more than living in a life-long process of recovery.

Freedom means we have passed through the recovery process and have been made whole.

Freedom is the Absence of Necessity: In recovery, we learn how to live with our condition without using.

The cause of our addiction remains, though it may have lost some of its power.

The outside of our cup is clean, but the inside is still dirty.

Just because someone stops using, doesn't mean they will no longer think like an addict or interact with others in the same way as active addicts do.

They may continue to employ the same old methods of control and manipulation to get what they want.

In freedom, the root cause has been faced, dealt with, and no longer exists.

The inside of the cup - our heart - has been made clean. When the inside becomes clean, the outside becomes clean also.

We stop behaving like active addicts.

Freedom is the Absence of Coercion: To coerce means to force someone to do something against their will.

We may want to stop using, but an overwhelming craving for more coerces us to continue. The absence of coercion means we can resist temptation. We are not powerless!

We possess the power of choice. We can take or leave our poison of choice. We choose to leave it.

That we are not powerless is true both for addicts and those who love them.

Freedom is the Absence of Constraint: The absence of constraint means nothing now holds us back from enjoying our freedom.

Instead of settling for the lifestyle we have been living, we begin to live the life we were born to live.

One of the problems with traditional recovery is the doctrine that once we're addicts, we'll always be addicts.

Though we have stopped using, we may still believe we will never be completely free and whole.

Traditional recovery tells us we will spend the rest of our lives in recovery.

That's like being stuck on an airplane that never lands.

Most addicts don't become free because they don't know there's anything beyond recovery. The "program" says freedom from addiction is not possible.

But it is!

There is another aspect to freedom we will discuss later; freedom in Christ.

ADDICTIVE BEHAVIOR
TAKES MANY FORMS

While our narrative focuses on drugs and alcohol, addictive behavior takes many other forms, potentially just as harmful to addicts and those who love them as substance abuse.

People can become addicted to food, sex, tobacco, shopping, shoplifting, gambling, thrill-seeking, gaming, pornography, cutting themselves, and many other behaviors.

No matter what form addictive behavior may take, it is rooted in the same sense or spirit of powerlessness.

We focus on substance abuse in the narrative, not because it is more important than the behavior you may be dealing with, but as a form of shorthand. A laundry list of addictive behaviors, repeated ad infinitum, would make this book hard to read.

If you or someone you love is addicted to a behavior other than substance abuse, simply substitute what you are dealing with whenever we mention substance abuse.

Most of the information in this book concerning substance abuse applies to all other forms of addictive behavior.

Whatever the behavior, this book can help you not only to recover, but to move beyond recovery to freedom, whether you are an addict, an enabler, or a member of an addict's family.

Recovery works best when all recover together.

Substituting One Behavior for Another

When one addictive behavior stops, it is not unusual for people in recovery to replace it with something else.

Someone who quits smoking may replace tobacco with food. A drinker may switch to gambling. Gaming and other forms of digital addiction may replace pornography.

We must be alert to the transference of addictive behavior from one expression to another.

One of the keys to recovery and freedom is to stop all addictive behavior long enough to allow the emotional issues driving it to surface. They can be dealt with after they surface.

If we continue to self-medicate to numb or avoid our emotional pain, our healing may be delayed or not take place at all.

Unless there's a miracle, and yes, miracles happen.

It is normal behavior for addicts to use.

It is a miracle when they stop.

Being in recovery is not supposed to be a life sentence. It is a process, part of a journey with a destination.

The destination is not recovery. The goal, if you choose it, is freedom.

There are going to be challenges along the way, but with the right kind of help and a determination to do whatever it takes, whether you are an addict or someone who loves an addict, you can become free.

One of the freest people on the planet!

SCIENCE, MEDICINE, AND MENTAL HEALTH

Researchers in science, medicine, and mental health continue to seek ways to solve the addiction puzzle.

We hope they succeed.

So far, some proposed new ways to conquer addiction have helped but still fall short.

They fall short because they do not address the sense or spirit of powerless driving addictive behavior.

They also fall short because too many researchers subscribe to the tenets of twelve-step recovery, despite forty years' worth of studies showing success rates for traditional recovery programs are only 5-10%.

One of these tenets is especially damaging; the idea that once people become addicts, they will always be addicts.

If researchers come to the table with a pre-conceived notion full freedom from addiction is not possible, they may not look for ways to set people entirely free.

Instead, their goal will be to help addicts achieve "tolerable recovery." That's a good goal. It's just an incomplete goal.

Tolerable Recovery

Tolerable recovery is good, but it is not complete. It allows us to function, but it does not make us whole.

It means we've stopped using, and we have learned to live with our sense of powerlessness and other distressful emotions.

Given a choice, people might prefer permanent freedom over tolerable recovery. Not knowing freedom is possible, most of us settle for the limbo of tolerable recovery and merely learning how to live with our pain.

Tolerable recovery does not set us free but renders us at least somewhat numb to our pain so that we may function reasonably well.

Achieving tolerable recovery often involves the long-term use of prescription medication.

Tolerable recovery is better than using. A chemically-induced calm is better than chaos, but merely learning to live with our pain is not the same as becoming free of it.

A counselor may encourage us to describe the circumstances, events, and relationships we believe caused our distress, and help us explore the painful emotions our memories evoke.

Regularly-scheduled mental health counseling sessions may continue for months or years; or until our insurance runs out.

In theory, revisiting the same stressful events and feelings, again and again, ought to desensitize us enough to achieve a degree of detachment; to numb painful memories and emotions until they lose their debilitating power.

But using this approach doesn't mean our distressful feelings have disappeared. They are still there, under the surface. We must continue to manage our emotional pain.

Because we can function, we may come to believe mental health therapy made us whole. Not knowing we can do better than function, we may settle for life-long tolerable recovery, until our pain breaks loose and surfaces again.

What happens if we are wrong about the source of our pain?

What if the events we recall, painful as they may be, are only symptoms or manifestations of deep-seated trauma?

What if the events we remember did not occur? False memories can lead us away from healing and into a dead end.

There's Plenty We Don't Know

Some people involved in traditional recovery may disagree, but we believe science, medicine, and mental health therapies can help people to at least stop abusing drugs and alcohol.

There's plenty we don't know about how our bodies, hearts, and minds work.

Is there a genetic predisposition toward at least some addictive behavior?

That's a question science may eventually be able to answer with a reasonable degree of certainty.

It may not apply to everyone, but if the answer is yes, then those whose genetic makeup sets them up for substance abuse can be warned and avoid getting into trouble.

Another area of research involves the exploration of the structure, chemistry, and function of the brain. We're all for it.

Research may very well uncover some of the physical/chemical causes of addiction and lead to the development of effective, multi-faceted, and individually-customized recovery strategies.

The Realm of the Spirit

Science and medicine can only take us so far. They cannot deal with the spiritual issues related to addiction and recovery.

Many scientists do not believe in God. They will not concede spiritual issues exist, or if they exist, that they matter. They discount any approach that includes a spiritual component.

That's a shame. We are willing to believe science and medicine can help. Why can't scientists and medical professionals extend the same courtesy to people of faith?

People have bodies, souls, and spirits.

The body is the tent of flesh we inhabit.

The spirit is that which gives us life.

The soul is what makes us individually unique - our character, gifts, personality, thoughts, emotions, memories, hopes, and dreams.

We must address all three - the body, soul, and spirit if we want to achieve permanent freedom and wholeness.

There is no rational reason that science, medicine, and people of faith cannot work together to bring hope to those who need it.

Choosing to use after a doctor tells us we are medically or genetically at a high risk of becoming an addict would not be a rational decision.

To use in the face of such warnings would demonstrate that a pervasive sense or spirit of powerlessness is already at work.

Scientific and medical breakthroughs are much to be desired, but they are unlikely to unseat the spirit of powerlessness as the root driver of addictive behavior.

Follow the Yellow Brick Road

Doctors prescribe medication to help people in emotional pain or with mental health issues to function normally.

Some people develop an addiction to their medication.

When doctors give emotionally-healthy people potentially-addictive medication to provide relief from chronic <u>physical</u> pain, the emotional root of powerlessness may be absent.

But if they continue to use these drugs, physical addiction may follow.

Patients seeking relief from physical pain may not exhibit an emotional predisposition for dependency when they start taking their meds. They may develop one if they continue to use them.

Stepping into the Void: When people can no longer get their pain medication from a legal and legitimate source, they may turn to the black market to find it.

If the meds they've been taking are unobtainable on the black market, they may turn to heroin or other illegal drugs for the relief they seek.

Despite attempts by some to deny it, there is a direct cause and effect relationship between over-prescribing medication and its availability on the black market.

> Richard: I was given a month's supply of an opioid after having several teeth pulled. I took one the first day. On day two, I switched to an over-the-counter pain reliever. A week or so later, I threw the rest of them away.
>
> Those pills had a street value of at least $750.00. Need I explain why legally-prescribed medication ends up on the streets?

51

Opioids Should Not Always Be the First Option: Research indicates opioids can be less effective than over-the-counter medications for pain relief purposes.

Perhaps doctors ought to recommend over-the-counter pain relievers before they resort to highly-addictive opioids?[10]

Instead of prescribing a thirty-day supply of opioids for people who may only need it for seven days, why don't doctors prescribe only seven-day's worth of pills?

Then there would not be nearly as many dangerous unused drugs sitting in medicine cabinets waiting to be stolen and sold on the streets.

In many places, heroin and fentanyl are cheaper, more widely available, and abused more often than black market opioids.

That does not excuse drug companies for recklessly promoting opioid use, drug wholesalers/distributors for filling ridiculously large orders, and doctors for over-prescribing them.

Welcome to Party Town!

During the ten years ending in 2016, drug distributors sold almost 21 million opioid doses to two pharmacies located in a West Virginia town with little more than 3,000 residents.[11]

There can be no plausible legitimate reason to ship so many dangerously addictive drugs to such a small town.
No rational person can believe none of these drugs would be abused or sold on the black market.

---

[10] *Evidence for the Efficacy of Pain Medications*, by Dr. Donald Teater, M.D., published by the National Safety Council.
[11] *Welcome to Williamson, W. Va., Where There are 6,500 Opioid Pills per Person*, by Gabe Gutierrez, Adam Reiss and Corky Siemaszko. NBC News, February 1st, 2018.

It is also hard to believe no one in the drug distribution chain noticed the volume of drugs flowing into this town was, to put it mildly, excessive.

We're talking about just one small town. How many other communities are drowning in a similar flood of addictive prescription meds?

As it turned out, one rogue Virginia doctor was responsible for writing 40% of those prescriptions.

The United States consumes far more opioids per capita than any other nation. We are the world's leaders in opioid use.[12]

How did it start? Why does it continue?

Follow the yellow brick road.

_____

[12] *The Surprising Geography of Opioid Use Around the World*, by Dan Kopf. Quartz Media, February 6th, 2018.

Medication in Recovery: A Good Idea?

Prescribed medication can play a decisive role in recovery, but its use ought to be more limited than it is at present.

Our current opioid addiction crisis can be traced in part to the aggressive marketing and over-prescribing of opioids for pain management purposes.

Step Down During Withdrawal: In the context of helping addicts stop using, medication can help manage the physical pain of withdrawal, and reduce the possibility of harm (including death), during the detoxification process.

Detoxification is a beneficial, well-targeted, and <u>temporary</u> use for medication.

Until only a few decades ago, most addicts kicked heroin the hard way: cold-turkey. They endured several terrible days of pain to break the physical addiction.

Today, pain management and medically monitoring an addict's condition during withdrawal is a blessing.

Some people in recovery circles are entirely opposed to the use of <u>any</u> mood-altering substance to help people recover.

They sincerely believe someone under its influence is not truly sober or clean. We only partly agree.

The long-term use of prescription medication can be beneficial if someone's physiological or psychological condition is severe enough to require it.

If the goal is not freedom, but achieving the ability to function, then medication can help. The meds may make them loopy, but loopy is better than dead.

It is better to function than not. Some people, short of a miracle, will never be able to do more than that.

Nonetheless, miracles are possible. We've witnessed them. We can always hope.

Trading Dependencies: Beyond breaking the power of physical addiction during the initial detoxification and withdrawal stage of recovery; or helping people with physical or psychological issues to function, the ongoing use of prescribed medication can be counter-productive.

A common strategy to eliminate a dependency on heroin is to replace it with methadone. Methadone may help people function, but all we have done is to replace a dependency on an illegal drug with a dependence on a legal one.

The black-market drug dealer loses a customer, but the clinic gains one. The money continues to flow, whether it's coming out of addicts' pockets, supplied by government agencies, or covered by insurance.

The root cause of addictive behavior remains untouched.

Heroin addicts are subject to the spirit of powerless; people who switch to methadone remain powerless.

If the goal is the ability to function, then the use of substitute medication is useful. If the goal is freedom, its use is counter-productive.

Interference with the Healing Process: The healing process requires us to feel and own our pain at various stages of our journey to wholeness. We cannot feel our pain to the extent needed while we are under the influence of medication that renders us emotionally numb.

To heal it, we need to feel it.

Substituting prescribed medication for illegal drugs can prevent healing. The emotional root cause of addiction is still present, unaddressed, unchanged, and waiting to flare up and drag us back into the pit.

People under the influence of prescription drugs may function, but they are not whole or free. They may be better off, but they are not better.

Tolerable recovery is good, but it is not complete. We may be managing or numbing our painful emotions, but they are still there.

Freedom is Complete

The healing of our emotions leads to freedom. Once we are made whole, we are no longer prisoners to past pain. Our memories of past traumas remain intact, but no longer drive us to crave relief or oblivion.

Freedom has many benefits. To mention only three:

- ❖ We resolve difficult situations instead of running away and hiding from them.

- ❖ We face and deal with painful emotions as they surface, rather than tolerate, medicate, or bury them.

- ❖ Traumas of the past no longer amplify painful emotions caused by injuries suffered in the present.

As good as tolerable recovery can be, we're not satisfied with stopping there.

We have no issue with those who decide to stay in recovery rather than move on to freedom. The choice is theirs.

We desire to break the power of all unhealthy dependencies.

We hope people will want to go all the way to full freedom.

Twelve-step recovery was once the only option available to those who wanted to stop drinking and using drugs.

That is no longer the case. Today there are many options from which to choose.

Recovery from addiction is no longer "one size fits all."

WHAT ABOUT A HIGHER POWER?

In our conversations with addicts, we have encountered two common complaints concerning faith:

The Pressure to Believe: The twelve-steps suggest that dependence on a higher power is necessary for a successful recovery. Turning our will over to the care of "God as we understand Him" is encouraged in traditional recovery.

Atheists and agnostics tell us they stopped going to meetings because they were tired of the pressure to believe in a higher power. People accused them of "not working the whole program" because they rejected "the spiritual aspect" of the program.

Censorship: All faiths are not always welcome in recovery groups. Some decidedly exclude at least one of them. Just to mention a particular deity's name is enough to set some people off.

When, in a meeting, Christians mention that Jesus Christ is their higher power, they can be angrily confronted and rudely treated.

Accused of "trying to force their beliefs on other people," they may be told to leave the group and not come back.

The use of force in matters of faith is anathema to us. Belief in God is a matter of the heart.

The authors of this book are followers of Christ, but we don't want to scare off atheists, agnostics, or people of other faiths.

We want everyone (not just Christians) to recover successfully.

Whatever you believe or don't believe, we hope you will read this whole book, so you can make a rational and informed decision concerning the information we present.

You may not agree with the spiritual content, but you may find the emotional issues we discuss useful and applicable.

Is Recovery Possible Without a Higher Power?

We believe recovery is possible without believing in a higher power.

There. We said it. Please don't shoot us.

This statement may upset some of our Christian friends, but that's okay. In a moment, we're going to upset our atheist and agnostic friends.

We are equal opportunity up-setters. We hope everyone has a sense of humor.

If recovery means we successfully stop using, and we do little or nothing beyond that, then recovery without belief in a higher power is possible.

However, we still face this reality; only one addict in ten who seeks help to stop using recovers. Only one addict in one hundred achieves lifelong sobriety.

Whether they did it without faith in a higher power is unknown.

Principles for Recovery and Freedom

Later in this book, we will introduce the six core principles of the *My Recovery Community*. Their purpose is to help people get free and stay free.

The first four principles help people achieve recovery, whether they believe in a higher power or not. People of any faith, or no faith at all, can follow them.

The last two principles are for those interested in moving on from recovery to freedom in Christ.

The fifth principle proclaims freedom for all is God's desire.

We can choose to reject the hopeless "once an addict, always an addict" creed.

The sixth principle discusses how accepting Jesus' offer of friendship can move us beyond recovery (and powerless, lifeless, religion), to empowering freedom in Christ.

Beyond Recovery

We are <u>not</u> talking about recovery when we talk about freedom, but about what lies <u>beyond</u> it. We are talking about what the Bible calls "freedom in Christ."

Our stance on freedom in Christ should satisfy our Christian friends. We also hope atheists, agnostics, and people of other faiths will concede the logic of this statement:

"Freedom in Christ is not possible without Christ."

ADDICTION AND INCARCERATION

Addiction and incarceration are closely linked, flowing from the same root of powerlessness.

The Third Year Itch

In our mentoring program for prisoners returning to free society after their incarceration, we consider someone successful when they stay off drugs, out of prison, and out of trouble with the law for at least three years after their release.

We define success this way because 80% of people in jail and 65% of those in prison, return to custody within three years of their release.[13]

Since 85% of crime is substance-abuse related, participants must also maintain their sobriety while they are with us.

Someone who reaches the three-year mark without committing a new crime is unlikely to return to prison. The three-year mark is also significant for people in recovery, though few seem to realize it.

---

[13] Bureau of Justice Statistics.

There Will Probably Be a Test

For many people, a critical test comes, often without warning, after two-three years of sobriety. People wake up one morning in terrible emotional pain. They don't know what is happening to them or why.

No one else seems to have a clue, either.

The only help our sponsors and peers in recovery can usually provide is to encourage us to stay the course. They are right, of course, but we need more than pat answers if we are to avoid relapse.

After two-three years of not using, the emotions we have been self-medicating to numb or avoid come to the surface. They are painful, more painful than we can bear.

We know how to stop the pain immediately. We can use.

Many do. But if we were better prepared for it, we could avoid relapse, face our pain, and come out on the other side in much better shape than when we went in.

We will explore this largely overlooked phenomenon (we call it "the moment of decision") later.

Bad Decisions

Most prisoners - 85% - are incarcerated because they make bad decisions. The decision to use is the most common wrong decision made by incarcerated men and women.

The average person living in "the free world" makes thousands of decisions a day, large and small. The average inmate makes only a few hundred decisions a day.

People who make bad decisions need to learn how to make good ones. The best way to learn is by doing.

Prisoners lose their power of choice. They cannot learn how to make better decisions by actually making decisions.

Our incarceration system doesn't teach responsible decision making. It mostly produces people who continue to make bad choices.

Our decades-old war on drugs is an expensive war we continue to lose.

One of the reasons we're losing: we're doing nothing to address the sense of powerlessness driving addictive behavior. If anything, incarcerating addicts reinforces it!

Another reason: we take people who make bad decisions, lock them up in a place where they make very few decisions, and expect them to make better decisions after we let them out!

To stop using and returning to prison, they need empowerment.

Instead, we take their power away.

It doesn't make sense, does it?

When viewed this way, the irrationality of our incarceration system becomes self-evident:

- ❖ Two-thirds of people released from prison keep coming back, serving life sentences on the installment plan.

- ❖ Too many people left prison with the same addiction issues they had when they went in.

- ❖ Most go right back to the same illegal activity they were engaged in before they were locked up.

Neither our criminal justice system, nor recovery programs based on the twelve steps, address the sense or spirit of powerlessness driving addictive, anti-social, and criminal behavior.

Until they do, our prisons and jails will remain full of people with addiction issues.

Addicts will keep on dying.

We'll keep spending vast sums of money on a lost war on drugs, instead of investing in approaches that have the potential to reduce crime and substance abuse.

Families will continue to suffer—especially children.

Justice requires punishment. Sanity requires facilitating a permanent change of heart and behavior.

These two goals are not mutually exclusive.

POWERLESSNESS:
THE ROOT OF ADDICTIVE BEHAVIOR

The root cause of addictive behavior is a pervasive sense or spirit of powerlessness.

It sits at the bottom of our emotional well, ready to pull us in and drown us.

It governs our attitudes and motivates our behavior. It produces emotional pain; often, more than any person can bear.

The spirit of powerlessness also produces uncertainty.

It may manifest as a sense of discomfort and unease, or a vague feeling something is missing or holding us back.

We cannot quite put our finger on what we're feeling or why. If we remain unaware a spirit of powerlessness is at work, it will continue to do damage.

The spirit of powerlessness is sneaky and ruthless. It creeps up on us until it infiltrates and affects every aspect of our lives; spiritual, emotional, and physical.

Most of us are unaware of its presence and influence, yet if we do not act to overcome it, it can hold us captive for a lifetime.

That most of us are unaware we may have become subject to a spirit of powerlessness is normal. We generally haven't a clue as to what drives our thoughts and emotions or motivates our behavior.

The theories we develop, the explanations we embrace as we try to understand why we think, feel, and behave as we do, are often inadequate or entirely off target.

Traditional recovery programs do not address the root cause of addictive behavior. They don't appear to know what it is.

If they knew a sense of powerlessness was the root emotional driver, no doubt they would have done something about it long ago, and recovery success rates would be considerably higher than they are.

Our Powerlessness is Real

Our sense of powerlessness is real. We are losing our power of choice:

The Loss of Personal Power: There are eras in history when people enjoy a great deal of personal liberty.

During other times, powers beyond our reach make decisions concerning the smallest details of our lives.

Human history is cyclical and repetitive. At present, there is a great deal of pressure worldwide on our liberties, and a corresponding erosion of our power of choice.

Power brokers and bureaucrats, known and unknown, now make decisions for us that only a short time ago we made for ourselves.

This disturbing trend largely escapes the conscious notice of a people distracted by a daily diet of bread, circuses, trivia, and feel-good.

Nonetheless, many people sense something is wrong.

Violence: Our sense of powerlessness is aggravated by what seems to be an increase in violence everywhere in the world.

The frequency and damaging impact of natural disasters, school and other mass shootings, ceaseless armed conflict throughout the globe, and ever more common acts of terrorism, give rise to a sense of powerlessness in many of us.

Information Overload: The ability to access news anywhere, at any time, on any number of devices, represents a significant step forward in the dissemination of information.

It also has unintended negative consequences.

The vastly expanded number of news outlets, an overwhelming volume of information, and our growing doubts concerning the trustworthiness of our news sources fan the embers of our unease.

Just as a steady diet of junk food can ruin our health, an overwhelming deluge of disturbing news concerning issues and events we cannot personally influence, or change, can have a debilitating impact on our attitudes, thinking, and emotional condition.

Pervasive anger deepens our sense of powerlessness and diminishes any sense of well-being we may still possess.

We can counter the effects of this matrix of negativity if we ration our use of social media, and exercise sound judgment concerning the sources of our information.

We can determine whether the news outlets we patronize are biased, in what direction they lean, and whether they follow an agenda beyond accurately presenting the "who, what, when, where, and how."

Unfortunately, finding news sources that give us "just the facts" without spin or ulterior motives is becoming very difficult.

So What? What does this have to do with addictive behavior and recovery?

Plenty. Disturbing global events, coming one right after another, circulated by a sensationalist media too quick to spread gossip and present opinion as hard news, have generated a growing mistrust of the news media.

We now live in a toxic worldwide environment where the spirit of powerlessness can thrive without impediment.

We are designed for peace but do not have peace. We live in a loud, crude, fast-paced, and dangerous world.

We have become slaves to a universal spirit of powerlessness.

Our Powerlessness is Not Real

It may appear to be a contradiction to say so, but our sense of powerlessness is also not real. To a fair degree, we still have the power of individual choice:

❖ We can control our consumption of news and other media. The phrase "garbage in, garbage out" comes to mind. We can lower the temperature by rationing our intake, being more selective about the news outlets we use, and being more discerning concerning their integrity and possible agendas.

- ❖ We can decide not to let things we cannot change upset or frustrate us.

- ❖ We can change our attitudes and control our emotions.

- ❖ We can treat others with civility and respect whether they reciprocate or not.

- ❖ We can love our enemies and forgive those who hurt us.

- ❖ We can deal with the personal issues preventing us from living a full, free, and peaceful life.

- ❖ We can decide to break the power of our addictions.

- ❖ We can serve others without any expectation of reward.

- ❖ We can determine whether the cost of our actions and responses is reasonable, and decide whether to pay it.

- ❖ We can say yes or no and mean what we say.

- ❖ We can ask for help.

Yes, we still have power. We can get out from under the spirit of powerlessness that enslaves us.

We can recover, and we can be free.

A spirit of powerlessness is
the root, but other factors
help set us up for addiction.

WHAT PRODUCES POWERLESSNESS?

While researching for this book, we met with more than three hundred people with addiction issues one-on-one or in small groups, to gather information and introduce the idea a sense or spirit of powerlessness is the emotional root cause of addiction.

Most were in recovery. A few were still using.

Their number one response? It makes perfect sense!

Many told us this new knowledge encouraged them. It clarified why and how they became addicts and gave them hope they could live an addiction-free life.

They wanted to succeed.

They were tired of being arrested and spending time in jail.

They were tired of relapsing and going to rehab after rehab.

They were tired of always being told they were powerless over their addictions.

Their families were tired of it, too.

Once we know the root of our problem, we can devise a lasting solution. Hope is a beautiful thing.

A Partial List of Influences

A spirit of powerlessness is the root, but other factors help set us up for addiction. We can't explore them all in just one book, but here are a few of them:

- ❖ Boredom
- ❖ Curiosity
- ❖ Peer pressure
- ❖ Environment
- ❖ Upbringing
- ❖ Toxic relationships
- ❖ Not knowing who we are, or why we're here
- ❖ An inability to connect with other people
- ❖ A failure to process loss
- ❖ Emotional traumas of the past.
- ❖ Fatherlessness

Fatherlessness

Western society currently suffers the effects of two epidemics: substance-abuse and fatherlessness. They are linked.

Fatherlessness is helping drive today's explosion of addictive behavior.

The years between 1960 and 2016 saw a more than 180% increase in one-parent households headed by mothers.[14]

The men who helped make the babies were, and still are, merely sperm donors - irresponsible, unsupportive, and absent.

---

[14] Between 1960 and 2016, households headed by single mothers increased from 8% to 23%, according to the *2016 Current Population Survey Annual Social and Economic Supplement*, published by the U.S. Census Bureau and the U.S. Bureau of Labor Statistics.

In the most egregious cases, the men come "home" for sex, to use or hide their drugs, or because they intend to exploit their children to get something for themselves, such as government benefits or a lighter prison sentence. Their kids are only props or accessories; otherwise, these men are uninvolved in their children's lives.

The absence of a loving, actively engaged father figure in the home is a significant indicator for future incarceration, substance abuse, poverty, educational underachievement, physical and mental health issues, and many other undesirable outcomes.

Single Motherhood is Tough: Single moms have an impossible job, the toughest in the world. They do the work of two people. They must be both a mother and a father to their children.

With only one income (good luck getting consistent child support from a missing, addicted father), the family suffers financially as well as emotionally.

The evidence shows that children do best when they have both a father and a mother in the home. Children with a loving, actively engaged father in the home:

- ❖ Are less likely to break the law, engage in addictive behavior, or indulge in early or risky sexual activity
- ❖ Do better in school and are less likely to drop out
- ❖ Tend to enjoy healthy relationships
- ❖ Tend to hold down high-paying jobs as adults
- ❖ Are less likely to become homeless or require government or charitable assistance
- ❖ Suffer fewer Adverse Childhood Experiences (have lower ACEs scores.)[15]

---

[15] *The Science of Dad and the Father Effect*, by Joshua A. Krisch, October 3, 2017. Published on fatherly.com.

Try as hard as she might; a single mother simply cannot do it all. It is challenging to shoulder all the responsibilities that ought to be shared by two parents.

Despite her best efforts, she may remain stuck in survival mode. The fight to keep the family together, especially under the pressure of poverty or near poverty, can eventually exhaust a single mother's spiritual and emotional reserves.

Assistance from government, charitable organizations, and other family members may ease her burden somewhat but can also do lasting, unintended damage. It can foster unhealthy dependencies.

Children who grow up with a single parent influenced by a spirit of powerlessness and the dependency it produces, are likely to pick it up themselves and carry it into adulthood.

They are likely to become manipulative, emotionally unstable adults, dependent on others to pay for their support.

Grandma Steps In: Sometimes, both parents are absent. To keep the children out of a government agency's hands, grandma becomes their mother.

In 2005, more than 2.5 million grandparents were raising their grandchildren, in large part due to parental incarceration and addiction issues.

That number has since grown to more than 3 million.

21% of grandparents caring for their grandchildren live in poverty; 26% are disabled.[16]

---

[16] From the Pew Research Stateline article: *Why More Grandparents Are Raising Children*, by Teresa Wiltz, November 2nd, 2016.

Years ago, mothers were the heroes who carried on when fathers were absent. Now mothers, under the one-two punch of addiction and crime, are turning their responsibilities over to their mothers.

Today grandma is the hero. She can't do it alone, either.

Grandparents who become the primary or substitute caregivers for their grandchildren must shift roles from being grandparents to being parents.

They lose out on being grandparents, whose only responsibility is to love their grandchildren and have fun with them. The grandkids miss out on the experience of having nothing but fun with their grandparents.

> Dawn: I was blessed to have four grandparents and five great-grandparents when I was growing up.
>
> The joy on their faces when they saw me and the love they gave me was a gift too few of the children we work with have enjoyed.
>
> I suspect it was a gift missing from the lives of many of our adults as well.

Grandparents have already raised a family; now, they must do it all over again.

At a time of life, when they should be able to relax and have fun with their grandkids, they must take on parental responsibilities.

It isn't fair to the grandparents, nor is it fair to their grandkids.

They may not have the energy to do it - but do it they must.

Identity, Meaning, and Purpose

Who am I? Why am I here?

Our sense of powerlessness begins with not knowing the answers to these two fundamental questions.

If we are going to live our lives with confidence, then each of us needs to know the answers; not just in our minds, but also in our hearts,

Without the strength and security that comes from knowing who we are, and the assurance of knowing we are fulfilling our destiny, we drift. Instead of proactively living our lives, we allow life to just happen to us.

We suffer a significant, painful loss. Know it or not, we mourn our loss. The spirit of powerlessness gains a foothold in our hearts and begins to weave its destructive web.

While it is possible to live a reasonably fulfilling life without having the answers to these questions, we are always much better off when we know who we are and why we are here. We may otherwise embark on an endless search for significance.

Or we may give up and give in to the spirit of powerlessness.

We may enjoy the blessings of a loving spouse, gifted children, many good friends, financial security, an excellent reputation, and other signs of a seemingly successful life.

Still, our relationships and achievements will be less fulfilling and meaningful than they ought to be, unless we know, in our innermost being, who we are, and why we are here.

We may gain the whole world but lose ourselves - our soul - if we are not rock-solid confident concerning our identity and purpose.

Richard: Back in the 1960s, my generation talked a great deal about "finding ourselves." Many of us dropped out of society and turned to drugs, thinking they would aid us in our search for identity and significance.

"Tune in, turn on, drop out" was our mantra. Tragically, many of us old, burned-out hippies have remained adrift over the decades since, and have passed our fears and uncertainties, lack of confidence, moral relativism, and self-centered philosophies to the generations that followed us.

We may be side-tracked into dead ends, neither uncovering nor fully deploying our gifts, unless we possess the answers to these two fundamental questions.

We may settle for scraps falling from life's table instead of having a seat at the banquet and enjoying a satisfying meal.

Conscious of them or not, unless we resolve our identity, meaning, and purpose issues, we will continue to suffer. In our search for relief, we may adopt destructive attitudes and become slaves to toxic desires.

The spirit of powerlessness takes over. Addictive behavior becomes a possibility.

We are supposed to know who we are and why we are here.

Not having the answers causes us pain.

A Case of Mistaken Identity

Many of us are confused about who we are. We have come to believe we are what we do.

When we meet someone, the first thing we ask is, "What is your name?" Then we ask, "What do you do for a living?"

We have their name and occupation. We think we know who they are and why they are here. We file the information away, or we forget it entirely. Others do the same to us.

When we don't know who we are, our occupation becomes our identity. The belief we are what we do can kill us.

Someone whose job has become their identity may work in their chosen profession for decades, possibly with one company, or more likely these days, for several - or they start a business of their own.

Then they retire in their sixties or seventies, in perfect health.

Six months later, they suddenly drop dead. Everyone wonders what happened.

When they lost their profession, they lost their identity. They no longer knew who they were.

Losing their sense of self killed them.

Created for Greatness

Our lives are supposed to count for something. Not knowing our purpose in life can cause us harm. Looking for meaning and purpose, we try a succession of things without committing to any of them.

Nothing works. Success eludes us. As we grow older, we feel the frustration and shame of repeated failure and defeat. A sense of powerlessness rules us.

We may become passive, doubtful of our ability to contribute to society in any meaningful way. "Nothing I do works or matters, so why bother?"

Believing our lives don't count; that we have nothing useful to contribute, adds to our sense of powerlessness. It is especially frustrating when we're sure we can be helpful, but our potential usefulness is not recognized by those who could put us to work.

Knowing why we are here invests our lives with power, gives us goals to reach for, and supplies the motivation to achieve them.

Even when life is difficult and challenging, it is almost always engaging. We may retreat when a battle goes against us, but we don't give up on life.

Whatever happens, we keep our eyes open for opportunities to share our gifts.

Knowing why we are here produces the drive to keep chasing our dreams. We walk through open doors or push on closed ones to see whether they might open. If they don't open, we may try to walk through them anyway!

People who know who they are and why they are here have power. People with power make things happen. Things happen to people without power.

Designed for Paradise

Powerlessness produces anger.[17]

Between the sense of powerlessness on the bottom, and the pervasive anger floating on the surface of our emotional well, we find a potpourri of other potentially damaging emotions; among them fear and anxiety, guilt and shame, hopelessness and depression. Just plug in your particular brand of poison.

These stressful emotions are often more of a burden than any one person can bear.

Our Creator did not intend that human beings would experience emotional pain. This great truth of the ages (mostly overlooked in these modern times), explains why we are so inept at dealing with our pain.

Our understanding of our inner selves is inadequate. We neither know why we hurt nor what to do about it. The best we can do is guess at the cause of our distress.

Our Creator is not a distant, unreachable, uncaring deity, or a force of nature. We are not supposed to be mindless cogs in a gigantic, impersonal machine. Our purpose in life has never been to suffer endless hopelessness, powerlessness, and misery.

We are supposed to live in a paradise, to enjoy everlasting, face-to-face friendship with the compassionate God who created us, to receive His love, live in it, and pass it along to others. We are supposed to live with passion and purpose - to be part of something greater than ourselves. We are supposed to love one another, be fruitful and multiply, subdue the earth, and rule it.

---

[17] We will discuss anger in the next chapter.

We are artistically and wonderfully hand-crafted, individually unique, creative, powerful beings, each with our unique gifts, personality, and character.

God made us in His image and likeness. We are reflections of His glory, destined to be filled with His love, and imbued with the power of His Spirit. Anything less than this ideal causes us pain.

Emotional Wounds

Too many of us settle for less than we can be, or what life can offer us. Aware of the reasons for it or not, we suffer loss and mourn our losses.

There are two types of painful emotional wounds. Trauma wounds are caused by damaging things done to us. Absence wounds form when we do not receive the benefits and blessings needed to grow, mature, and be whole.

Trauma Wounds: Childhood traumas can produce an emotional vulnerability that opens the door to a spirit of powerlessness, especially if power was taken from us by an act of emotional or physical violence.

> Richard: I was kidnapped and sexually assaulted by a relative at a very young age. While I was too young at the time to understand what had happened to me, I sensed it was not good or right.
>
> The trauma wound created by this one-time act robbed me of my power in a shockingly intimate way. It pierced me to the core of my being.
>
> I suffered long-lasting damage, years and decades of pain, fear, anger, self-doubt, and depression. I also became subject to a spirit of powerlessness.

I was truly powerless. I was too young to understand what had happened to me and too small to fight back. A man who was supposed to love and protect me betrayed me in the worst possible way.

I will share more about this experience and its outcome later. For the moment, you should know this story has a good and powerful ending.

Absence Wounds: Emotional and spiritual damage can also occur through the absence of good things that every human being needs but does not always receive - especially love.

People suffering from absence wounds may have a vague sense something is missing, but they will generally be unable to work out what it might be.

Trauma wounds are challenging enough to get to; absence wounds can be even harder to uncover.

When we search for a trauma wound, we search for something concrete enough to find.

With an absence wound, we are looking for something that did not materialize.

Nonetheless, we can find them. We can heal. We are not without hope or resources.

Not knowing our discomfort and our addictive behavior comes from a spirit of powerlessness, gives it free rein to continue its destructive work.

Knowing that a sense of powerlessness drives our addictive behavior is the beginning of our empowerment.

ANGER: OUR FIRST RESPONSE TO POWERLESSNESS

After a moment of disbelief, our first response to loss, including the loss of our power, is anger. We may not be aware we are angry, but it is there, all the same, waiting for an excuse to explode.

A sense of powerlessness sits at the bottom of our emotional well. Pervasive anger sits on top.

Powerlessness produces anger.

Anger is a secondary emotion, ranging in intensity from mild annoyance to violent rage. It doesn't stand on its own. Anger floats like an oil slick on top of other painful emotions.

Anger shields us from feeling our underlying pain.

It is easier to be angry than to feel powerless, hurt, abandoned, ashamed, excluded, unimportant, or any other painful emotion we might mention.

That is why we ought to uncover and work on the underlying emotions that drive it, rather than try to heal our anger.

After we deal with its cause, pervasive anger disappears.

85

False Power

We may use outbursts of anger to control people or keep them at a distance. Angry outbursts are expressions of <u>false</u> power.

We feel powerful when we erupt, especially when the people around us cower or hide, but after the drama is over, we remain just as powerless as we were before we exploded. We may also lose power.

Our outbursts alienate family and friends. They may conclude our temper is too volatile, and our ability to exercise self-control too weak to guarantee we won't explode again. Consequently, they avoid or cut us off entirely.

No one wants to be the target of our explosive temper. No one wants to walk on eggshells or tiptoe around us, fearing we're liable to go off at any moment.

Healthy versus Unhealthy Anger

Healthy anger is an immediate, proportional response to an offense that quickly comes and goes.

When our anger is healthy, a minor offense will produce a small response. The response to a sizeable transgression will be more intense. Wherever it is on the intensity scale, we get over our anger quickly. We soon forget about whatever set us off.

Unhealthy anger is chronic; it is always present, bubbling below the surface, ready to erupt for any reason or no reason at all.

Chronic anger may begin as early as infancy and continue to grow throughout an entire lifetime.

People who feel and express healthy anger are <u>not</u> angry all the time.

Their anger is a healthy, proportional response to an incident or a sudden loss. Emotionally healthy people get angry, get over it, and move on.

People stuck in unhealthy anger are different; they live in a state of <u>constant</u> irritation, even wrath. They hold on to anger and won't let it go.

Things that trigger their outbursts may have nothing to do with the real reasons they are angry. They are only convenient excuses to justify blowing up.

Whether we are aware of it or not, or willing to admit it or not, too many people in our society (and around the world) are angry to some degree most of the time.

We're angry because our freedom of choice is increasingly compromised, and we don't like it.

Robbed and Angry About It

Our loss of power is real. We <u>are</u> being robbed.

How do you feel when you realize someone has robbed you?

When someone rips us off, we may experience a momentary shock of disbelief. We cannot believe it happened to us. Then we get angry.

Anger is a normal response to loss. Almost all of us will be a victim of crime at least once. For most, it is a memorable event, a once-in-a-lifetime experience. We get angry; we get over it, we move on.

But what if being robbed is an almost constant and persistent state of affairs?

Healthy anger is like accidentally cutting our self with a knife; a quick, sharp, pain; a wound that heals quickly. It hurts, but we clean and bandage it. Finally, only a small scar may remain to remind us of our mishap.

Instead of a knife cut, imagine someone took sandpaper to your arm, made a couple of quick passes with it, and then left your arm alone. The next day they do it again. And again. And again.

One little one-time scratch may not do a lot of damage, but a little light scraping, digging a little deeper day after day, doesn't give your arm a chance to heal. A severe wound will eventually develop.

That is what is happening in our society. We live in a state of constant irritation and abrasion.

Every pass of the sandpaper, every disagreement, every robbery, every injustice, every time we feel disrespected or taken for granted, every time we're offended, every time our power of choice is compromised.

Every time we believe we are powerlessness.

We don't have a chance to heal. Our anger doesn't dissipate.

Instead of getting angry and getting over it, we stay angry. We become stuck in our anger, and we can't move on. We're not fighting occasional battles, where we win some and lose some. It's fight or flight all the time. Our emotional meter reads Defcon One.

Our adrenalin pumps until our spiritual and emotional reserves are exhausted. We're primed and ready to explode. One more relatively minor irritant may be all it takes to set us off.

We are anxious and angry, surrounded by people just as frustrated as ourselves. It's a potentially explosive mixture.

A Matrix of Noise, Conflict, and Violence

Perhaps you remember when Sunday was a community-wide day of rest? Most stores closed for the day. People relaxed.

We still miss the tranquility of that weekly day of rest.

Whether people were churchgoers or not, everyone enjoyed the peace of an entire day of relative inactivity.

Sunday rest provided a welcome respite from the hard work and pressure of the other six days, but now it is gone. We are the poorer for it.

We have become accustomed to living in a matrix of constant strife, noise, discord, and disrespect.

The resulting lack of peace and rest is harmful to our spiritual, physical, and emotional well-being.

We have collectively become like the proverbial frog in a pot of cold water. The water is gradually heated until it begins to boil.

The frog doesn't realize it's in trouble until it's too late.

Constant noise, activity, and conflict make us uneasy and angry. It twists our emotions until we don't know what we're feeling or why.

The pressures of modern life increasingly turn us in a negative, selfish, and cynical direction.

We seek relief and rest and cannot find it. We'd like to escape altogether, but we cannot afford to quit our jobs and run away to paradise.

In the absence of joy and inner peace, we settle for the false comfort of substitutes, the destructive coping mechanisms of drugs, alcohol, and other addictive behaviors.

"Get Off My Road!"

When people are angry as a rule; when our anger is as pervasive as it has become; when many of us are prone to be offended, it is easy to trigger frequent angry outbursts.

Take road rage. Road rage occurs because we are already angry - <u>before</u> we get in the car.

We feel powerful behind the wheel of a big machine. We are powerful.

We can go anywhere we want to go. We may not have control over much of the rest of our lives, but at this moment, we're the king or queen of the road. The road is ours; it belongs to us.

Then someone cuts us off in traffic. That other driver has just robbed us of our power.

Anger rises. Our reason goes out of the window.

We retaliate. We tailgate the offender, flash our headlights, honk our horns, and hurl curses at the total stranger who just invaded our little kingdom.

We take risks we would not take if we were rational. We speed up to pass, no-passing zone be damned. We flip our enemy the bird as we fly by. We almost clip their front bumper as we pull back in front of them.

We suddenly slam on our brakes and force them to slam on theirs. We've just taken back our power and taken away theirs.

If both vehicles come to a stop, a physical confrontation may take place.

In our unreasoning state, we don't pause to think about what we're doing, why we're doing it, or whether someone could be hurt.

Instead, we are obsessed with getting even (though we call it justice) and taking back our power.

This kind of anger is neither healthy nor normal. Emotional pressure has built up over time and not been relieved. We don't express our anger in a manner proportional and appropriate to the offense, nor do we get over our anger anytime soon.

We don't take a moment to remind ourselves the incident that triggered our anger is not nearly important enough to ruin our day or rob us of our peace and sense of well-being.

Given our emotional condition, we may not have a sense of peace or well-being to lose.

A rational person would conclude the other driver is an idiot, stay away from them, and let them go on their merry, oblivious way. Instead, we allow our pent-up rage to explode.

We may have won a battle, but when we lost our temper, we lost the war. We handed our power over to someone we will never see again.

We let a stranger steal our power and ruin our day!

Intolerance and Rage Have Gone Mainstream

Pervasive anger has become the matrix of our lives.

We cannot let go of it, as we could easily do if we weren't under the influence of a spirit of powerless.

Instead of letting go of things that upset us, we store every offense in our hearts. We keep a detailed record of offenses against us. We add more names to our list of enemies.

No wonder we have more addictive behavior, more shootings and violence, and a more polarized social/political environment today than at any other time in recent memory.

Pervasive, society-wide anger has been sneaking up on us for decades, and now it is here.

Road rage is not the only manifestation of the rising tide of anger in our society. We have nearly lost the ability for rational, calm conversation, or vigorous, yet respectful debate with those with whom we disagree.

We have become intolerant of the smallest, most insignificant differences. We are unwilling to listen or compromise.

We have lost our joy, and we have no peace.

We have replaced diplomacy and tact with slander and name-calling. We are becoming a nation of squalling infants in adult bodies.

We no longer find unbridled rage confined to the fringes of society. It has invaded what once was the comparatively calm, rational center. We are losing whatever self-restraint we still possess.

We have a universal issue with anger, whose root is a sense or spirit of powerlessness.

Some people are "anger addicts." Anger can be a form of self-medication. An outburst sometimes makes us feel better.

Endorphins released during outbursts attach themselves to the opiate receptors in our brains, providing a measure of pain relief, and producing effects like those produced by opiates.

When we ask someone whether they feel better after an angry outburst, the answer may be "yes!"

Other Reasons We Get Angry and Stay Angry

A sense of powerlessness is the root of chronic, unhealthy anger, but other influences also come into play:

Injustice: When we are victimized, our rights are violated, or we become aware others are maltreated, our sense of justice and fair play is offended.

Misunderstanding: We misinterpret what someone says or does, or we don't understand why something is happening.

Frustration: Frequently recurring bad experiences may bring on or reinforce a sense of having lost control.

Pride: Anything that interferes with our getting what we want, or challenges our good opinion of ourselves, may make us angry.

Learned: We may have learned anger from the behavior of our parents, siblings, other family members, or friends. If they had short tempers, we might develop one, too.

Ways We Sin in Our Anger

Angry people are angry for a reason; often, an excellent reason.

Anger itself is not a sin, but we may sin while we are angry. Here are a few ways we take our anger too far:

Verbal, Emotional, or Physical Abuse: We take our anger out on others, often people who have nothing to do with the reason we are angry. They just happen to be there when we explode. We may also take our anger out on people who are trying to help us.

A person who seems kind and polite may be hiding and storing their anger. Rather than direct an angry outburst at someone who may retaliate with a similar expression of wrath, they may blow up on someone "safe."Someone who loves them.

Manipulation and Control: Anger can be a tool to get others to do what we want, such as doing our chores for us, or getting a free restaurant meal. Rather than face our wrath, people will do what we say.

Vengeance: We get even with people whom we believe have harmed us. We may go to war against the entire world. Seeking revenge is a misguided attempt at self-empowerment.

Someone took our power away. We want it back. Striking out at our enemies makes us feel powerful. Gaining revenge may feel good at first, but it solves nothing. It leaves us no better off than before, and often, worse off.

Our desire for revenge may also set off a destructive cycle of getting even that only ends with someone's death.

If we succeed in getting even, we will discover it didn't change anything. We're still angry - and stuck.

Deception: We keep our plans for revenge to ourselves, while we maintain an appearance of friendship. We tell people we've forgiven them and behave in a friendly manner toward them.

They believe us until we strike without warning!

Two Ways We Express Anger

We Blow Up: We explode in an angry outburst without regard for the consequences or other people's feelings. We shout, scream, throw things, punch holes in walls.

Everyone knows we're angry.

We Clam Up: Also known as "the silent treatment." We get quiet and erect an emotional wall.

We rattle the pans while cooking dinner and punish people with a brooding silence. We are unresponsive to questions or comments beyond a few grunts or monosyllabic replies.

Anger Management

Society's answer for rage is anger management. Anger management is good, but it is not a permanent solution.

Gaining the ability to manage our anger does not mean we are no longer angry. The root of our anger remains. We're still angry. We have only learned to control our outbursts.

The ability to manage our anger may sometimes delay or work against our healing. Our new-found ability to control the urge to bite someone's head off may lull us into believing we've solved our problem, and are no longer angry.

Self-control is good, but healing the emotions driving our rage is better. Gaining the ability to control our outbursts is better than having no self-control at all. Managing our anger prevents us from harming others or saying or doing things we may later regret.

Managing our anger can also require an awful lot of work.

Healing Our Anger

What can we do about our anger?

On a macro, society-wide scale, probably not much. It would take a large-scale miracle to turn society's temperature down.

However, we still have the power to deal with our anger on a personal level. The antidote for pervasive, unhealthy anger is forgiveness.

We may know we ought to forgive those who hurt us, but we may not know how to forgive.

We may also find it difficult to tell the difference between really forgiving someone, and only stuffing our anger back in its box.[18]

We can be set free of unhealthy, chronic anger, and deal with the underlying emotions that cause it, including powerlessness.

We can learn how to forgive, and to know when we have forgiven someone. When we are angry, we no longer deny it. We walk through it until we get to forgiveness.

As we become whole, our anger evaporates. A day will come when we won't have to manage it because it will be gone!

---

[18] Anger and forgiveness are subjects the *My Recovery Community* addresses in depth.

MORE REASONS PEOPLE USE

As we have seen, the root emotional cause of addictive behavior is a sense or spirit of powerlessness.

Powerlessness is the root, but there are other influences at work:

Hedonism

Why are we surprised addiction is an issue when our popular culture glamorizes selfish, destructive, and even dangerous attitudes and behaviors?

Naïve young people are especially vulnerable. Their brains are still developing, and their life experience is limited.

They trust people they should not trust.

We do not teach them how to read between the lines. They don't realize they are nothing more than targets to those trying to sell them something.

Sophisticated marketers exploit them.

The "Everyone Does It" Lie

Whether it's substance abuse or some other destructive behavior, users want us to believe "everyone does it." That's supposed to make it acceptable and desirable.

Running a few anti-substance abuse ad campaigns to counter society's pervasive "if it feels good, do it" philosophy, and expecting it to work, doesn't cut it, either.

It Could Be Worse: Most active substance abusers believe that everyone uses. The mistaken belief their behavior is common and normal helps them justify their drug use.

The facts indicate otherwise:

❖ 24.6 million people, representing less than 10% of the U.S. population ages twelve and older, abuse drugs or alcohol.

❖ 19.8 million of these, or 7.4% of the U.S. population, smoke marijuana.[19]

While these numbers represent many potential tragedies in the making, substance abusers are very much in the minority as a percentage of the total population.

Addiction is a problem, but we can be thankful it is still limited to a relatively small, though a significant number of persons.

_____

[19] *National Institute on Drug Abuse*, from a survey conducted in 2013 by Substance Abuse and Mental Health Services (SAMSA)

Affinity Groups Share Common Interests: Everyone does <u>not</u> do it, but everyone in a user's social circle probably does. As with any affinity group, substance abusers tend to hang out with people who share their interests; in this case, other substance abusers.

As their addiction takes hold, being around non-users makes them uncomfortable. To avoid being challenged about their drug use, addicts drop their relationships with non-users. They replace family and friends who do not use with people who do.

Take a Pill. Take Another One.

Many people who suffer chronic physical pain or emotional distress turn to medication for relief or escape.

The United States and New Zealand are the only countries that permit drug companies to advertise directly to consumers. An immense volume of advertising encourages consumers to request specific drugs for pain relief purposes.[20]

There's a lot of money to be made selling pain meds, whether over-the-counter or by prescription.

Meds Cost Less than Addressing the Issues: No one in the industry who wants to keep their job will admit it, but insurance companies would rather pay for pain management drugs than more costly surgery or mental health therapies.

Feel bad? Take a pill. Trouble sleeping? Take a pill. Trouble waking up? Take a pill. Trouble living? Take a pill.

---

[20] Ad spending by drug companies topped $6 billion in 2017 (Source: *Kantar Media*).

Type two diabetes? Don't change our eating habits to lose weight and lower our blood sugar levels; take a pill, especially the ones that cost hundreds of dollars a month.

When the pills stop working, we can inject insulin for the rest of our lives. The drug industry will be happy to sell us the insulin, injectors, and test kits.

Do we have an emotional issue such as anxiety? Why work to uncover and heal the cause, when we can take a pill for instant relief?

A Slippery Slope: It's a tiny step from following the dosage instructions on a pill bottle, to taking "just one more" to find relief. From there, it's another small step on the road to addiction; doctor shopping.

After we run out of doctors willing to give us a script for our meds, we enter the black market.

Tilulae Regina

A few years ago, a pain management clinic opened in our city. It was an immediate success.

The clinic was a cash-only enterprise - they did not accept insurance or government benefits. A doctor's visit took five minutes, fifteen minutes for first-timers. Fifteen minutes to diagnose a condition requiring "treatment" with highly addictive medication.

Most of the clinic's customers came from out of state. Most of the prescriptions the clinic issued were filled in other states.

Have dope, will travel.

In one year, this doctor wrote more than 8,000 prescriptions for approximately 3,500 people, a total of almost 600,000 pills. More than 80% were for Oxycodone.

Neighbors complained about the increased traffic, parking issues, and other clinic-related problems until the authorities acted.

The doctor accepted a plea deal. She lost her license to practice medicine. The clinic closed, the neighborhood returned to normal, and the customers moved on to find other drug suppliers.

Just one rogue doctor prescribed almost 600,000 opioids in one year. And we wonder why opioids have become a problem!

There are plenty of doctors out there doing the same kind of damage. There are plenty of drug companies willing to supply the drugs.

How to stop it? We've started to lock up doctors who over-prescribe dangerous medication; perhaps we ought to charge the officers and board members of the drug companies that supply the drugs.

A few manslaughter convictions and some seriously hefty fines ought to be persuasive.

Until the law caught up with her, this "doctor" was proud of her contribution to the destruction of lives.

She had forgotten the part of the Hippocratic oath that reads, "First, do no harm."

Postscript - the vanity license plates on this doctor's car read:

"TILULAE REGINA." That's Latin for "PILL QUEEN."

Using to Regain a Sense of Power and Control

Another, lesser-known reason we use is to regain a sense of control over our lives; to take back the power to make our own decisions.

The Decision to Use is Empowering: We may lack the power to influence or change the big "x" decisions made for us, but we can still make smaller "y" decisions.

For many people oppressed by a spirit of powerlessness, "y" is a decision to engage in some form of addictive behavior.

We can choose drugs, alcohol, gambling, sex, shopping, smartphones, gaming, overeating, or any number of other behaviors.

Research for this book included conversations with hundreds of active and recovering addicts. The answers to one question were telling:

"The last time you used, did you feel 'better' when you used, or when you first decided to use?"

Almost everyone responded, "When I made the decision."

For most, a sense of relief and empowerment comes, not when we use, but when we <u>decide</u> to use.

There is frequently a lag time between deciding to relapse and actual relapse. After we choose to use, unless we already happen to have what we want on hand, it takes time to find a dealer or get to a liquor store.

The decision to use is a poor choice, but it produces a desirable result. The decision to use restores a sense of being in control. It counteracts our sense of powerlessness.

Recapturing a Lost "First Love" Feeling

Using feels good, or at least it does at first. That's why we indulge, especially if we don't usually feel good.

Our problems disappear or at least seem manageable. For a little while, we're on top of the world.

Then we come down, and it's back to our painful, powerless reality. But now we know how to escape. We use again.

If using didn't feel good, the first time we used would be the last time we used. But in the beginning, it does the job. We continue to repeat the experience. Eventually, using becomes a lifestyle, a regular part of our daily routine.

From Feel Good to Feel Normal: Over time, the pleasure becomes less intense than it was at first, especially if we're using a drug that causes a tolerance response. If we continue down the path long enough, the pleasure fades away until it disappears.

We've entered a new phase. Now we use just to feel normal.

Feeling normal doesn't last long. We're on a slippery slope, well on our way to destruction.

From Feel Normal to Feel Nothing: If we do not stop, we enter the next phase. We can no longer reach normality. We begin to experience the reality of Richard Farina's 1966 novel, "*Been Down So Long, it Looks Like Up to Me.*"

We continue to believe we're not addicted. Other people may get hooked, but we're different. We can handle it. We can stop anytime we like. It's just that we don't want to. But we could.

We cannot admit to the reality of our condition, but people who love us can see we're in trouble. When our non-using family members and friends intervene to prevent our self-destruction, we don't listen.

We cannot listen. We're not ready to acknowledge the pain driving our addictive behavior or face the damage we're doing to ourselves and others.

To face reality is too painful, too much of a blow to our pride.

We're not listening to anyone. We won't let anyone help us unless it's "help" that enables us to keep using.

False Hope: We need more to satisfy our cravings. We are never satisfied because there is never enough. We're heading in the wrong direction.

Down.

But we keep on going, even after the pleasure is long gone.

Why? Because we "live" in the false hope the next time will feel as good as the first time. It seldom does. But we continue to chase that "first love" feeling nonetheless.

Sometimes we recapture it. The first love feeling comes again for a moment. But then it's gone. We continue to pursue it until the chase takes us out.

Only one addict in ten seeks help to stop. Only one of the ten addicts who get help manages to stop using. That means only one addict in one hundred makes it.

What happens to the other ninety-nine? Prison, a mental health facility, or death by overdose or other preventable causes.

This picture is bleak. We can, and must, do better.

An Inability to Process Loss

An inability to process loss often leads to addictive behavior.

You may be familiar with the stages of grief and loss. These are not linear; that is, we may not pass through them in the order they are given. We may skip some of them altogether.

A grieving person may also experience two or more stages at the same time.

Our responses to loss are not bound to these stages. Every person deals with loss in a unique way.

The stages of the grieving process are not a to-do list:[21]

The Loss: Someone we love dies, a meaningful relationship ends, we lose a job; these are a few losses that cause us pain.

The loss itself is usually not included as one of the stages of grief and loss. It ought to be. Unless we suffer a loss, there is no reason to grieve.

Shock and Disbelief: Most people call this stage "denial." Tired as we are of "river in Egypt" jokes, we call it disbelief.

People who suffer loss don't necessarily deny something terrible has happened. We're just in shock. We have a hard time believing it when we first learn of it.

It's shocking to learn someone we love is gone, especially when we can say, "I was just talking with them yesterday!"

---

[21] *My Recovery Community* offers help and support to people going through the grieving process.

Anger: We've lost someone or something important to us, and we do not have the power to change history.

Feeling powerless makes us angry.

We may also be angry at the person who died or divorced us, or at whoever deprived us of something we valued.

Bargaining: We set conditions for dealing with our loss and moving on with life.

We tell ourselves and others, "When they catch the guy who did this, then I will feel better." They catch him. We don't feel better.

"When he is convicted and goes to prison, I will feel better." He's convicted and imprisoned. We don't feel better.

"After they execute him, I will feel better." Eventually, he meets his maker. Years, and sometimes decades have passed since he committed his crime, but we still don't feel better.

"If he falls on his knees and begs for my forgiveness, then I might forgive him."

The bargaining stage is not a good place to be stuck, but many people get stuck here. Forgiveness releases us from bondage to those who hurt us.

Deep Sorrow: Bargaining is often followed by deep sorrow as the reality and permanence of our loss sinks in. We are inconsolable during this season.

If we've lost a loved one, we may feel guilt over things left unsaid or undone.

If any well-meaning soul is going to say something stupid such as "I know how you feel," this is when they will do it.

The best comfort anyone can offer during this time is an empathetic silence or a heartfelt "I'm so sorry."

The story of Job comes to mind. After the loss of his children and all he possessed, his friends came to see him. At first, they sat with him in silence; but when they began to speak, they said foolish and unhelpful things.

In one of the best examples of sarcasm in the Bible, Job finally said to them:

"Truly, you are the people, and wisdom will die with you!" [22]

Reflection: Some call this the depression stage. Depression may very well be part of the grieving process. Deep sorrow begins to ease, and we can reflect on our loss without feeling overwhelmed by grief.

Some people may begin to hint we ought to be "over it" by now.

Ignore them. Time does not heal all wounds, but its passage can help us reflect on the good times we shared with our absent loved one without falling into a seemingly bottomless pit of grief.

Acceptance: Some people call this stage "closure." There is no such thing as closure.

We have sustained a loss. It is often a permanent loss.

Our loss never goes away. It becomes part of our history, part of us. The reality of our loss is not going to change. It will remain open.

---

[22] Job 12:2

What will change is how we feel about it. While we may no longer be in deep sorrow, we will, from time to time, recall our loss with a mixture of longing and peace. Time does not heal all wounds, but it can bring us comfort.

Recovery, Rebuilding, Redefining: As we come to terms with our loss, we begin to redefine our life within our new reality.

We may find another job after losing our previous employment, change our name after a divorce, or decide we would like a toaster instead of a toaster oven after a spouse passes away.

> Dawn: My father often says his name changed after my mother died. For more than forty years, his name was "Les and Arlene Carroll." He had to become used to just being "Les Carroll."

> My mother preferred toaster ovens over toasters, so that was what sat on our kitchen counter. My father preferred toasters, but he deferred to my mother's preference.

> After Dad passed through the grieving process following my mother's death, he bought himself a toaster.

Outward and seemingly small changes like this demonstrate the presence of inner peace and acceptance of our loss.

Difficulty processing loss is normal. The length and depth of our grief will generally be proportional to the magnitude of our loss.

The loss of a parent, a job, a home, marriage, freedom, and so on, will require going through a grieving process. Our sense of self and our customary way of life may also radically change.

We can use all the encouragement and support we can get to come to terms with our loss and move on with our lives. We don't have to collapse under a load of grief. We do not have to relapse.

WHY OUR KIDS START USING

We asked incarcerated adults how old they were when they started using. Most told us they began to use around the age of eleven.

Since this is the case, measures to prevent children from using should start considerably earlier.

There are many reasons kids start using. We cannot possibly cover them all. We will cover some of the most important ones.

Powerless from Birth

Children may develop a sense of powerlessness because they start life <u>without</u> any power. Adults make all their decisions for them, beginning before they're born.

Pre-Natal Irresponsibility: Parents' risky behaviors and poor lifestyle choices before a baby is born can harm a child's health, well-being, and hurt their potential for success.

Expectant mothers who want healthy babies should not use.

Tragically, many do. Children then pay for their mother's addictive behavior, sometimes for a lifetime.

Overbearing Parental Authority: From birth until age eighteen, adults make almost all their decisions for them, even tiny ones (eat your peas).

Very young children need a high degree of adult supervision to ensure their well-being and safety. Parents <u>should</u> make most decisions for them.

But parents are not always aware of how their children feel about being bossed around. They do not always recognize when children are ready to make at least some decisions on their own.

A sense of powerlessness may gain a foothold as children grow older if their parents continue to treat them like babies.

To prevent powerlessness from taking hold, parents should appreciate their children's growing competence and permit them to make age-appropriate decisions.

Parental Neglect: Children living with addicted parents often suffer a damaging deficit of care. They are frequently left to feed and take care of themselves and their younger siblings.

Hunger is a common condition among the kids in our *My Club* mentoring program. We feed them.

In our community, free food is readily available for needy families; but some parents are simply not willing or able to prepare three meals a day.

Other parents may do a good job providing for their children's physical and educational needs but pay little attention to their emotional and spiritual needs.

Spiritual and emotional neglect gives powerlessness the key to a child's soul. Addiction is likely to be part of their future.

Many addicts started using at the age of eleven. In practical terms, we have less than ten years to ensure a child doesn't fall prey to a sense or spirit of powerlessness and begin to engage in addictive behavior.

Parental Choices: Decisions parents make for themselves, and their families, can have a profound impact on their children:

- ❖ Dad takes a new job in another city. The children must move away from their friends, school, and extended family.

- ❖ Mom and Dad separate or divorce. Their children must now alternate between two parents and two homes.

- ❖ Mom is an addict. She is arrested, convicted, and sent to prison. Her children are farmed out to relatives or placed in foster care.

Children's lives, for better or worse, are disrupted. They are at the mercy of their parents' choices. Parents rarely consult with them about these changes. They must go along, even if it hurts.

Adverse Childhood Experiences (ACEs)

A significant risk factor for future substance abuse, Adverse Childhood Experiences (ACEs) include:

- ❖ Physical, sexual, or emotional abuse

- ❖ Physical or emotional neglect

- ❖ Witnessing violent acts involving their parents or caregivers, including violence directed at their mother by her partner

- ❖ Substance abuse in the home

- ❖ Mental illness in the home
- ❖ Parental separation or divorce
- ❖ Incarceration of a parent or other household member

These experiences reinforce a sense of powerlessness. Kids are powerless to do anything about them.

Studies indicate 28% of children with significant ACEs scores experience physical abuse. 21% are also sexually abused.

Parental divorce and separation rates and the frequency of substance abuse are also high.

Almost 40% of children with ACEs scores have experienced two or more ACEs, and 12.5% have experienced four or more.

ACEs have a cumulative, as well as an immediate adverse effect.

Researchers found children with high ACEs scores experience lifelong health, social, and behavioral problems in adulthood, including involvement in addictive behavior.[23]

One Child's Story

A pre-teen boy was seated at the dinner table, enjoying a peaceful meal with his family. Then he politely asked whether he could have a second slice of pizza. An adult friend of the family yelled at him just for asking for one.

The boy responded in anger and ran from the room. It took several hours to calm him down.

---

[23] Information about ACEs can be found on the Centers for Disease Control website: cdc.gov

Earlier that day, he had learned his mentor, one of the few positive male role models in his life, was being deployed to the Middle East. He bottled up the pain of this loss and carried it all day.

Mealtimes had been peaceful all week until the adult who started the disturbance joined them that night. There was plenty of pizza, enough for everyone to have several slices.

Remember - he didn't just help himself to a second slice. He politely asked first. His reward for good manners was an unexpected and unfair verbal assault.

This boy lived with several adults who routinely yelled at him, sometimes all of them at the same time. He was often the target of their anger and a scapegoat for their sense of powerlessness.

A child grieving the sudden loss of his mentor did not get the empathy and support he needed. He kept his pain to himself, only exploding after an adult yelled at him for no reason.

After living with angry adults since birth, this young man has severe physiological and psychological issues. He is finally getting professional help.

People do what they know to do. When a home is not peaceful; when adults routinely yell at their children, kids learn how to defend themselves - or escape.

The adult may be the initiator and aggressor, but the child will receive the punishment if they respond in anger.

The child can't win. They don't merely feel powerless; they are powerless. That's a set-up for future substance abuse.

This boy's story is not unique. Too many parents are too busy and too tired to engage in the subtleties and effort involved in raising emotionally healthy children. They have only enough strength to regulate their child's outward behavior.

Many parents raise their kids the same way their parents raised them. If they grew up in a dysfunctional emotional cycle, they are likely to pass their dysfunction on to the next generation.

It takes effort and patience to understand what is going on in a child's heart and get to know who they are. The goal of too much parental discipline is to ensure their child behaves:

"Just don't embarrass me, kid."

Drama, chaos, and oppression is hardly a good foundation for a healthy, productive future for any child. Unfortunately, it is a familiar dynamic in far too many families.

Their Parents Use

Children who live in homes where substance abuse is common are at considerable risk of also using. Too many children have at least one parent who has spent time in prison or jail for substance-abuse related reasons.

Without compassionate, long-term intervention and care, they will follow their parents into the same destructive lifestyle. Once they are in it, they have less than a 10% chance of getting out.

Curiosity

Do you remember dreaming about your future when you were a child? Children can't wait to grow up. They want to know what it is like to be an adult. They dream about what their lives will be like when they are twenty, thirty, and forty years old.

Young people are innately curious. Everything is new to them, and anything is possible. They want to experiment, to try new things.

Hopefully, experimentation will help them become all they were born to be. Unfortunately, some of the things young people try can lead to their destruction.

Kids see adults around them doing "adult" things and want to try them, too. They're in a hurry to grow up.

They are just as interested as adults are in feeling good.

Social and Peer Pressure

Kids are subjected to a constant flood of messages, both subtle and overt, encouraging them to engage in so-called "adult" behavior.

With the now-widespread use of social media by children, these messages are more pervasive and compelling than ever.

Adults have a difficult time resisting the lure of the screen. Kids are just as vulnerable.

Hypocrisy: Many in the media industry claim their program content doesn't influence anyone to do anything.

These same people then sell advertising by persuading clients their commercials will influence buyer behavior!

They get away with this hypocritical stance hoping no one will notice the contradiction.

Outside Guidance and Support: When parents fail to gently and firmly guide their children and do not invest time and ongoing effort to know and understand what they are thinking and how they feel, kids will find guidance and support elsewhere.

Children get a lot of information about how the world works from their just as naïve and inexperienced peers. Some of their friends may be somewhat street smart, but most are not.

Teens believe they are ready for anything. Their immaturity and inexperience make them easy targets for predators.

If one of their friends uses, tells them it feels good, and has the means to get high on hand, they may give it a try.

It takes a lot of inner strength, maturity, and a strong sense of self to resist peer pressure.

Kids who feel powerless may not have what it takes to resist temptation.

"If it Feels Good, Do It!"

Why are we surprised when young people use alcohol and drugs and engage in other risky behavior?

They are only responding to the dominant message of the popular culture that engages and targets them:

"If it feels good, do it!"

The glamorization of substance use, outright lies (smoking weed and vaping are harmless), and the promotion of self-indulgent lifestyle choices are only a few manifestations of the "if it feels good, do it" doctrine.

Our culture encourages young people to do whatever feels good while ignoring or downplaying the consequences of such selfish, self-destructive behavior.

Faith calls them to a higher purpose: to be loving, generous, and unselfish.

Given the tidal wave of self-indulgent messages and the relative trickle of empowering life-affirming ones, young people are hard-pressed to choose wisely.

What could possibly go wrong?

"That's So Old School!"

Kids want to be hip, attractive, and grown-up. They believe it when society makes getting high seem hip, appealing, and adult.

Today's kids are not any smarter or more knowledgeable about life than previous generations were at their age.

They may have access to better technology and more information, but that doesn't mean they are better equipped than their elders were, at the same age, to deal with life's challenges.

Living in a digital world with their heads bent over a smartphone renders many young people less aware of their surroundings, and less able to distinguish between reality and non-reality.

They may not acquire the life skills they need to live in the real world. Heaven help them if the power grid ever goes down.

Ignorance is Not Necessarily Bliss: We worship at the altar of youth. It's a mistake. Young people may be intelligent, but intelligence is not all they need. They need knowledge and the kind of wisdom that comes with real-life experience.

Rudimentary familiarity with history would also help. People who couldn't be bothered with history rarely appreciate how much the past influences their daily lives.

They do not grasp how much they owe to those who came before them. Without historical context, each generation tends to believe it is the first to have all the answers.

Hippiedom? Hippie Dumb: Many of us who came of age in the sixties rejected the wisdom of our parents and grandparents.

We ignored the positive aspects of tradition. We attempted to do what we thought was brand-new: create a utopia.[24]

We were told not to trust anyone over thirty. We believed our parents, teachers, pastors, and other authority figures were the problem. We were sure they didn't know what they were talking about, especially when it came to sex, drugs, and rock n' roll.

They were the "Greatest Generation" who survived the Great Depression, fought World War II to stop fascism, and built the world's most robust economy.

While it still hasn't reached everyone at the bottom of the socio-economic scale, many in our generation enjoy the prosperity our forebears created.

---

[24] In 1516, Sir Thomas More coined the word "utopia" and published a book by the same name. Few realize utopia means "no place" or "nowhere" in Greek.

We still don't get the joke. Sir Thomas sent us on a fool's errand. We have been looking for "nowhere" for the last five hundred years!

Back then, we didn't appreciate it. Some of us still don't.

In our arrogance, we thought we knew better than they; that the older generation knew nothing. We believed it because we were younger and thought we were smarter.

In our ignorance, we believed older people who had sacrificed a great deal for our sakes were only out to spoil our fun.

The same message is still being preached today to a new up and coming generation. It is an ancient message. It is a lie.

If we had bothered to study history, we might have realized our new ideas were not new. People had tried them before.

And they had all failed.

When we rejected almost all our parents tried to teach us, we missed out on the many benefits that come from drawing on the wisdom and experience of our elders. We had to relearn it the hard way.

Now we are the older generation, the old school senior citizens who know nothing.

Hopefully, we have learned from the foolishness of our youth. If so, we can pray our children and grandchildren will believe us when we tell them, "It's not a good idea to go there."

A Lack of Unsupervised Outdoor Play

A fundamental shift in childhood experience has taken place in recent years. This change is one of the factors driving addictive behavior among the current generation of young people.

It has contributed to the spread of the spirit of powerlessness many people are subject to today.

Kids spend significant time at home, at church, at school, and in other places where they are closely supervised by adults who tell them what they can and cannot do. When they misbehave, these same adults punish or discipline them.

This part of the childhood experience has not changed.

If children do not receive consistent adult supervision, nurture, and discipline, they may not acquire the self-discipline, patience, manners, work ethic, empathy, and a host of other social skills and attitudes they need to become mature adults.

If they spend too much time under overbearing adult authority, they may become angry, resentful, rebellious, and emotionally damaged. They may become unproductive and dependent, rather than interdependent, contributing members of society.

The Change: What has changed in recent years? We've all but lost a significant relief valve and learning process.

Not long ago, kids spent a significant amount of time without adult supervision playing outdoors (on days it didn't rain) with their friends.

Not anymore. Visit many family neighborhoods today, and you will not see what we used to see on holidays, weekends, and after school - lots of kids playing outdoors with other kids. Now they are indoors playing with technology.

Why is this a problem?

Playing outdoors provided hours of relief from the constant control of adults. It gave children the freedom to explore, invent, and make their own decisions. It taught them how to settle disputes with other kids.

They invented games, established the rules, and enforced them, without any adult help at all.

Indoors, they were under adult authority. Outdoors, kids were free and powerful.

What caused this change? Video games, computers, tablets, and smartphones.

Let the Mayhem Begin: Lt. Colonel Dave Grossman, a retired Army officer, and professor of military science has written extensively about the negative impact of what he calls "murder simulators" on the young people who play violent computer games.[25]

Grossman outlines an issue the military has faced for centuries; most human beings have an inbuilt reluctance to shoot at other human beings. They train soldiers to overcome it.

Forensic studies of Revolutionary and Civil War battlefields show, on average, only one soldier in ten fired his weapon! The other nine went through the motions of loading and firing but did not shoot. They found one rifle with nine unfired rounds in the barrel!

The military solved this problem by replacing bull's eye targets with human silhouettes. By the Vietnam War, firing rates had improved significantly.

With the introduction of computers, law enforcement and the military began to use first-person shooter computer simulations in their training, leading to further improvements in firing rates.

Grossman points out the simulations used to train the military and law enforcement are nearly identical to the first-person shooter computer games kids play, with one big difference:

---

[25] You may be interested in two of his excellent books: *On Killing* and *Stop Teaching Our Kids to Kill.*

<u>There is no moral component built into the computer games kids play</u>.

Military and law enforcement trainees learn to shoot only at the bad guys. If they fire at a civilian, they fail the test.

Not so with the games, kids play. They can mow down as many people as they like without suffering consequences.

When the game is over, they start a new one. All the people they killed come back to life.

Excessive gaming has become a form of addictive behavior.

The computer game industry denies their games have any effect on whether children shoot up their schools or perform other acts of aggression and violence.

Computer games make kids who feel powerless in real life feel powerful. In first-person shooter games, they possess the power of life and death.

The same sense or spirit of powerlessness that drives addictive behavior also motivates mass shooters to kill.

Many of today's kids do not spend nearly as much time as they used to out in the neighborhood, unsupervised, hanging out with their friends, physically active, doing their own thing, and making their own decisions.

The decline of this essential means of escape from adult authority means kids are making fewer choices on their own as they grow up.

Too many of our children do not learn how to exercise their power of choice while they are still young, setting them up to make bad choices as adults, such as engaging in substance abuse.

Conversations with Kids

Many years of one-on-one conversations with kids reveal the following:

- ❖ Most tell us their parents and other adults talk <u>at</u> them, but do not listen <u>to</u> them.

- ❖ Adults tell them what to do, but rarely ask what <u>they</u> want to do, or how <u>they</u> feel about things.

- ❖ They live in one world, and their parents live in another. They connect on the surface, but rarely with sustained intimacy.

Christian Kids: Kids growing up in Christian homes experience additional challenges, especially if their parents are church or ministry leaders.

People expect them to be in church whenever the doors are open and to behave themselves.

People hold them to higher standards of conduct than other kids. If they transgress, they are judged not only by their parents but also by other members of the congregation:

"You're the pastor's daughter. You're supposed to know better!"

Busy with the ministry, church leaders sometimes fail to give their children at least as much attention as they give to others.

Ministers often say our families come before our ministries. Our words are empty if, in practice, we consistently put the needs of our flock ahead of our children's well-being. We know at least one teenager who asked his father, a prison minister:

"What do I have to do to get your attention - go to prison?"

Parental Faith: Too Strict or Too Shallow

Too many Christian parents hold their kids to the impossible standards of a particularly legalistic version of the faith.

When parental discipline prioritizes punishment over guidance, it may only produce proper behavior for a season. In the end, it will breed rebellion rather than the fruit of heart-felt love.

At the other extreme, parental faith may be inconsistent and shallow. Mom and Dad may behave one way at church and another way at home. They say one thing but do another.

Children are keen observers of their parents' behavior and attitudes. They know many of the secrets their parents try to hide. Parents may be shocked at just how much they know.

Here are some of the things Christian kids tell us:

"My parents are hypocrites. I don't want to be like them."

"If Christianity isn't real to my parents, why should it be real to me?"

"When I'm eighteen, I'm out of here. No one will make me go to church."

Given these sentiments, parents should not be surprised we lose so many of our children when they leave the nest.

Proverbs 22:6 Raise a child in the way they should go, and when they are old, they will not depart from it.

If we want our children to enjoy a consistent, authentic, life-long relationship with God, keep them from becoming slaves to the spirit of powerlessness, and avoid addictive behavior, then we ought to make sure our faith is more than cosmetic.

Lip service to God is not enough.

If our faith is deep and real, our children may reject it for a season, but in the end, God will draw them back. If our faith is shallow and phony, it may take a miracle to bring them home.

There are two kinds of Christians: Christians of culture, and Christians of faith.

Cultural Christians go to church for any number of reasons, but faith's deeper meaning eludes them.

But for Christians of faith, Christ is a solid foundation. They cannot conceive of living without a total commitment to Him.

If we want our children to believe, then we ought to examine ourselves. Is our faith shallow, cultural, and powerless? Or in-depth, meaningful, and powerful?

We are dealing with a dangerous spirit of powerlessness.

Which kind of faith is most likely to defeat it?

Sin Feels Good

One of the problems with persuading children to forgo using drugs or alcohol, is we do not tell them sin feels good.

Perhaps we fear they might be more likely to experiment if they knew it felt good? In an attempt to protect our kids, we lie to them by omission or commission.

Keeping Our Youthful Foolishness Secret: We may think it's a good idea to wait until our children reach the threshold of adulthood before we tell them about the dumb things we did when we were young.

It isn't a good idea. Our warnings to avoid harmful behaviors ought to include our own experiences; otherwise, our kids may ignore our advice.

Disregarding what we say, one of our kids decides to use. They discover using feels good.

The result? Every adult authority figure who warned them about the dangers of substance use loses their credibility.

Compounding the problem is the young person's new attitude:

"How can anything that feels this good be wrong? My parents, teachers, pastor, etc. don't know what they're talking about."

Tell Them the Truth. Tell Them Early: We cannot lie to our children about substance abuse. We ought to tell them using feels good.

We should also explain that's the nature of the trap. It feels good at first, but after that, it's all downhill.

It is a good idea to tell our kids about the dumb things we did, including our use of drugs and alcohol, when we were young,

We should talk about it while they are still young.

Remember, most addicts start using by age eleven. We need to establish our credibility well before they reach that age. If we wait too long, it may be too late.

Kids get a lot of misinformation from their friends about alcohol, drugs, and many other aspects of modern life. By the time parents sit down with their kids to discuss these things, they may find it's too late.

Their children already think they know a lot more about the subject than mom and dad.

What We Did: Before we were married, we decided we would not hide our past foolish behavior from our children. It was one of the best decisions we made.

Our children grew up hearing about things we did when we were young, including their dad's alcohol and drug abuse, and their mother's struggles as an enabler.

Our kids were neither shocked nor traumatized about our past. Our stories were part of their growing up.

Being honest about our past mistakes and their consequences, meant using drugs and alcohol held no fascination for them when they entered their pre-teen years.

From a very early age, they understood we knew what we were saying. We never lost our credibility. We admitted our mistakes and acknowledged our struggles to overcome them.

They listened when we shared our stories with others. They watched as we dealt with our issues, persevered through difficult times, and lived out our faith in front of them.

We were not perfect parents, but it helped our children that we were open about our past.

They never developed a "we know more than you do" attitude.

They listened to us and believed what we said.

Aren't children too young to hear about these things?

We believed whatever our kids were too young to understand would go right over their heads without causing them harm.

We decided if they were old enough to ask about something, then they were old enough to get an answer. It worked.

> Dawn: Our kids grew up in a loving and peaceful (for the most part) home. Richard and I did not yell at each other, though I must confess to having a pretty good temper when our kids were younger.
>
> My temper came from my pain and powerlessness. My children saw me fight for my healing. I admitted my faults and apologized to them when I was wrong or unfair.
>
> Despite our shortcomings, our children became loving, peaceful adults. We are proud of them. We asked our daughter once how we ended up with her the way she is.
>
> She told us:
>
> *"You did not raise me in a Christian home. You raised me in the presence of God."*

There's No Such Thing as "Quality Time"

To prevent the spirit of powerlessness from gaining a foothold in our children's lives, we ought to spend lots of time with them.

Children need <u>quantity</u> time with their parents.

We should not ration love and positive attention. Children need plenty of both on an ongoing, consistent basis.

There's no such thing as <u>quality</u> time.

The quality time concept is only an excuse to justify spending less time with our children than they need or deserve.

What Kids Know: Children don't know the difference between quality time and quantity time. They have no idea the limited time they spend with mom or dad is quality time.

All they know is they are less important than whatever is keeping their parents from spending lots of time with them.

If all they get is so-called quality time, kids may not feel valued or loved. They will feel powerless to persuade their parents to spend more time with them. When they are older, they may not care whether mom and dad spend any time with them at all.[26]

It takes quantity time to demonstrate genuine love and maintain healthy relationships. It takes quantity time to raise a child to become spiritually mature and emotionally whole.

A child who does not receive the positive, life-affirming attention and consistent discipline they need, may misbehave to get attention.

---

[26] Listen to *Cats in the Cradle*, a song by Harry Chapin.

To a child who craves love and nurture but doesn't receive it, negative attention is better than none. Without intervention, anti-social behavior may become a lifelong problem.

Annoying, whiny, self-centered children may become annoying, whiny, self-centered adults.

There is no such thing as quality time.

Failing to Empower Our Kids

Parents can prevent the spirit of powerlessness from taking root in a child's life by giving them age-appropriate decision-making power.

Most people learn by doing. Kids need to learn how to make good decisions while they are still young by making decisions.

Letting their children make decisions while they are still young and living at home, allows parents to monitor the choices they make, guide them when they make bad ones, and protect them from the worst consequences of bad decisions.

Everyone makes mistakes. Some do not learn from them.

Parents can ensure their children do.

If children do not learn to make wise decisions early in life, they are likely, due to inexperience, to make poor choices as adults.

Resentment: If a child is not allowed to make some of their own choices, resentment may result. If the parents' inability to let go of power continues, resentment may become anger, and anger, bitterness.

Bitterness shuts off communication and damages relationships.

Resentful kids who feel powerless do not trust their parents with their thoughts, feelings, and activities. They keep secrets from them, but they share them with their friends.

They will turn to their peers for advice and support; friends who may also be frustrated with their controlling parents.

A secret society excluding adults is born. Welcome to the generation gap.

There are choices a sixteen-year-old can make that a ten-year-old may not be ready for, or a ten-year-old can make that a five-year-old cannot.

Determining when a child is ready to make age-appropriate choices is more art than science. It has more to do with maturity than with age.

People make thousands of decisions every day, both large and small. Not everyone is good at it, particularly if we did not learn how to make good decisions while we were young.

It can be hard for parents to give up control, but it is necessary if we want our children to become mature adults. Our prisons are full of people who don't know how to make good decisions.

Self-Diagnosis: Allowing our children to make age-appropriate decisions has another benefit. If a child makes a poor decision while they are still under their care, parents can help them diagnose what went wrong. They can learn from the experience.

We allowed our children to make more of their own decisions as they grew older, and it paid off. Sometimes one of them wanted to do something we weren't sure they were ready for, but after talking it over, we decided to let them try.

If they succeeded, we knew they were mature enough to make those kinds of choices.

And if it didn't work out as we hoped? Then we helped them diagnose what went wrong. We asked questions:

"What do you think happened?"

"What might you have done differently to change the outcome?"

"If you tried it again, what would you do differently?"

> Richard: I had conversations like this with my son. When something didn't work out, Jimmy was always very quick to figure out why.
>
> Sometimes he tried again, doing things differently. Other times he concluded it was a bad idea, and there was no need to do it again.
>
> In the end, the two of us always had a good laugh:
>
> *"That didn't go very well, did it, son?"*
>
> *"No, it didn't."*
>
> *"But you'll do better next time."*
>
> He always did.

Some parents are good at letting go of the power to control every aspect of their children's lives. Others are not. Some parents are themselves too emotionally damaged to let go of power. Others do not let go out of fear for the children's safety.

To prevent a spirit of powerlessness from taking root and leading them into addiction, it is vital children acquire the power to make their own choices before they reach adulthood.

Adults who feel powerless use.

Kids who feel powerless may become adults who use.

BEGINNING OUR
JOURNEY TO WHOLENESS

Why do addicts use? As we have seen, these are the most common responses to an underlying sense of powerlessness:

- ❖ Self-medicate to avoid or tolerate our emotional pain

- ❖ To regain power or gain a sense of having power

- ❖ To recapture that "first love" feeling.

Since a condition of the heart motivates addictive behavior, the solution to addiction is a <u>change</u> of heart.

Human behavior begins in the heart. If our hearts are wrong, then our thinking will be wrong. If our thinking is wrong, then our behavior will also be wrong.

We can change our thinking and our behavior through a sheer exercise of the will - but no amount of will power can change our hearts. When our will weakens, we will relapse.

We can change our thinking and behavior through twelve-step recovery. Still, until it deals with the sense of powerlessness driving addictive behavior, the best we can hope for is tolerable recovery.

133

We may successfully stop using without experiencing a positive change of heart, but the root of our problem will remain. We can expect future relapse.

Raising Our Expectations

Most people choose recovery over freedom because they are unaware they can be completely free. Most programs tell us a lifetime "in recovery" is the best we can achieve. They tell us once an addict, always an addict.

Tolerable recovery is good. It is better than using, but it is not complete. Freedom is complete.

Recovery or freedom? What's your pleasure?

Just as no one recovers alone, no one becomes free alone. We need plenty of help from family, friends, mentors, other people in recovery, and God to find freedom.

Our journey to recovery begins the moment we admit we have a problem, and we become willing to do something about it.

Our journey to freedom begins the moment we accept Jesus' offer of friendship.

It is possible to recover without believing in a higher power. It is not possible to enjoy freedom in Christ without Christ.

Jesus is the Healer; He knows what is in our hearts, and He knows how to make us whole. He is also willing to make us whole.

As our journey to freedom progresses, the powerlessness driving our addictive behavior will lose its grip on us. Emotional traumas of the past will lose their power to hurt us.

We will become powerful through the Holy Spirit.

Talk Without Action is Just Talk

Whether you are an addict or someone who loves one, our journey begins with the recognition we have a problem.

For addicts, this means admitting we are addicted.

For family members, this means we cannot continue to blame the addict in our family for everything that has gone wrong.

For addicts, family members, and friends alike, accepting personal responsibility for "our stuff," and a willingness to do what is necessary to change, is essential.

Many of us manage to admit we have a problem, but then do nothing to solve it.

Because we have talked about a problem, we may believe we have done something about it. Not so.

Talk is helpful, but talking alone rarely solves anything. Without action, talk is just talk.

We also ought to realize our addicted family member is not the problem. They are only part of the problem. Just as no one recovers alone, no one gets into trouble alone.

We got into trouble together. We recover together.

Three Life Stages

There are three stages of life. Ideally, we pass through the first two and live most of our lives in the third:

Childhood/Dependency: The moment we are born, and for years afterward, we are entirely dependent on our parents and other adults for everything we need.

During this early time of life, we learn good manners and other social skills. We begin to acquire the fruitful heart attitudes every person should possess before adulthood: love, joy, peace, patience, kindness, goodness, gentleness, faithfulness, and self-control.

If we are to become mature and responsible adults, the nine fruit of the Spirit must become ingrained in our character.

We are too young to make big decisions, but with parental guidance, we can learn how to make small ones.

Teenage/Independence: By the time we reach our teens, we are physically, but not emotionally ready for physical intimacy.

Our hormones are flowing, but our brains are still developing.

Ideally, the fruit of the Spirit is now well established, reflected in our character, attitudes, and behavior. Self-control is critical at this stage of life.

Our decision-making ability continues to develop. We need less adult supervision than before, as we demonstrate competence and responsibility.

We have dreams and plans. Our lives lie before us; anything is possible.

Our eagerness to become full-fledged adults may lead us to ignore what adults try to teach us. Believing we're ready for adulthood, we forget we still need guidance from people older, wiser, and more experienced than ourselves.

We have been dependent until now. Now we want to swing to the other extreme; to be independent, free of restraint, and adult supervision.

Our lack of experience makes us vulnerable to con games and exploitation. We have not yet acquired discernment. We believe we are indestructible.

Death is a far-off possibility. Besides, only older people die.

We are not old.

We do not yet know who we are, nor why we are here, but have begun our search for identity, meaning, and purpose. It's a time to experiment; to try new things.

Adulthood/Interdependence: By now, we know who we are and why we are here. The fruit of the Spirit has become an integral part of our nature and character.

We have learned empathy and are concerned about the welfare of others. Our concern does not stop with sympathetic talk. We act to make things better for people in pain.

We are no longer dependent as children are, nor are we independent as teenagers believe they are.

We have learned to be interdependent. We are part of the fabric of family, friendship, and community. We are contributors, part of something greater than ourselves.

We have a healthy appreciation for our gifts and do not engage in false modesty about them. We do not need to possess so-called self-esteem because we know our true worth.

137

We appreciate the encouragement of others, but do not chase after approval and affirmation.

We do not run from emotional issues or challenges. We face and deal with them as they surface.

We do not let pride keep us from reaching out for help when we need it.

Stuck: Some people become adults in their twenties; others not until their thirties or forties, and some - never.

Addicts become stuck in the dependent/childhood phase or the teenage/independence phase. They don't play well with others.

Life is all about them. They are selfish and immature. They are adept at manipulating others to get what they want. They are usually incapable of genuine love, but they are good actors.

They are likely to fake love to get what they want. The people they allow into their lives have only one purpose; to serve and be useful to them.

Once someone is no longer useful, they end the relationship, often abruptly.

Unstuck: Emotionally healthy, spiritually mature people are not prone to indulge in addictive behavior, nor do they allow addicts to manipulate them. They possess power but are not interested in controlling or ruling others.

Their relationships are healthy. When a disagreement occurs, they do not allow it to fester, nor do they gossip or complain about people with whom they have conflicts.

They engage quickly and directly, doing what they can to broker a peaceful, mutually-beneficial resolution.

Oppressive Authority

Authority becomes oppressive when it is too controlling, too involved in the smallest details of our lives. It robs us of the ability to make all but the most trivial decisions.

Oppressive adult authority during our childhood and teen years opens the door for a spirit of powerlessness to take root.

Depriving children of opportunities to make age-appropriate choices sets them up for later addictive behavior.

If we have an angry, sullen child or teenager living in our home, they likely behave that way because they feel powerless.

The reason may be a situation outside the home, such as being bullied in school. It may be resentment over unreasonable rules at home, or because adults do not listen to them.

A stable, loving home, where there is excellent communication between family members, and where children feel free to talk and are listened to, can prevent a spirit of powerlessness from taking root and growing.

Selfishness in Recovery

When we start attending recovery group meetings, we may hear we are supposed to be "selfish in our recovery." That is not quite right.

Addicts already believe it's all about them. The family may make their addicted member the center of attention as well.

Such thinking is counter-productive. People who love addicts also suffer. They deserve as much attention and consideration as addicts receive.

Recovery should be every addict's number one priority, but not at the expense of their relationships with family members and friends.

Others have suffered and paid for their selfish behavior. The sooner we can stop the pain, the better for all concerned.

Addicts should never use being in recovery as an excuse to continue to hurt, ignore, or manipulate those who love them.

Our recovery and our relationships should both be our top priorities. They should have equal weight and attention.

Addicts are selfish by nature. Continuing to be selfish will hinder our recovery. If we want to recover, we need to become less selfish. Our recovery will not be real until we begin to care about other people.

The family members and friends of addicts may be frustrated and angry about their seeming (and quite likely, actual) continued selfishness.

They have waited a long time for their loved one to stop using.

They are impatient for things to get back to normal.

If things were ever truly normal, it is going to take time before family members begin to see the good old days return.

One of the best things they can do is seek help for themselves.

If family members focus on an addicted family member's recovery and neglect their own, they are likely to be bitterly disappointed when relapse occurs.

Remember - no one recovers alone.

THE MOMENT OF DECISION

Many people in recovery face a moment when no power on earth will keep them from relapsing. We call it "the moment of decision."

If it is going to happen, it will generally be within the first three years of our sobriety or abstinence. We call it "the moment" because it does not last long, though it may seem to go on forever while we're in it.

It often begins with sudden, intense emotional pain. To manage or avoid the pain, many people relapse when it hits. While it may not happen to everyone, we try to prepare people for it, just in case.

What Is It?

Many of us use so we do not have to feel whatever emotional pain we may be in or deal with the circumstances that produced it. Getting numb helps us avoid or tolerate our pain.

Then we stop using. We have just ceased doing the one thing that kept our pain at bay.

We have changed our behavior, but our emotional issues remain, mostly untouched, below the surface.

141

Some people sail through the early years of their recovery without experiencing the moment. Theirs appears to be a gradual, less dramatic release from pervasive emotional pain.

Others wake up one day in unexpected, terrible distress. For those of us who experience the moment of decision, it generally takes two-three years of not using before the pain we were running away from comes to the surface.

When it comes, we don't know what is happening to us. One day we felt fine; the next, we hurt so badly we think we're going crazy!

We're up and down, experiencing high highs and low lows. The pain has our complete attention.

We reach out to our friends in recovery for help, but no one seems to know what's happening to us. They tell us to hang on, and it will pass.

They are right. It will pass, but the support our friends offer may not be enough to get us through it. The pain, the intensity, and insanity of it seem to go on forever, even though it may only last a few days or weeks.

Hard on Others: The last thing we need when we are hurting is to be dumped on by self-righteous people with all the answers.

Brace yourself; it is likely to happen.

Some Christians will interpret the sudden onset of pain as a "lack of faith," a result of "unconfessed sin," God's judgment, or evidence of spiritual immaturity.

They will not be shy about saying so. These folks will quote the Bible, telling us what to do and what we should have done.

It is almost a given they will gossip.

This experience may cause us to feel isolated. The "help" these people offer may feel like judgment.

It is judgment Thank them politely, then move on. Find <u>real</u> help.

Be glad most Christians will not behave this way. They will be caring and supportive.

Hard on Ourselves: We may judge our being in pain as a failure of faith on our part, or if we dare allow ourselves to think or say it, God's failure to be faithful.

Your pain is not a matter of faith or a lack thereof. It is a normal part of the healing process. As crazy as it may seem, your pain is a sign of God's love for you.

Hebrews 12:6 For those whom the Lord loves He disciplines, and He scourges every son whom He receives.[27]

Our pain is real and intense. It seems as if there's no end in sight. We cannot endure it. It hit without warning, and we were unprepared.

We know how to stop the pain immediately. We can use. We can numb ourselves again and stuff the pain back in its box.

Whether we relapse or not in response to our pain, we still don't understand what happened to us.

No one told us this was coming, so we were not ready for it.

---

[27].Hebrews 12 is the Bible's great chapter on trouble and its purpose.

How Do We Prepare?

We can do better than just survive it. If we prepare ourselves to walk through the pain instead of running away from it, we will come out on the other side stronger and closer to true freedom than we were before everything hit the fan!

Here are three things we need to be ready:

- ❖ Friendship with Jesus that goes well beyond mere religion.

- ❖ A mentor. A real one.

- ❖ Friendships with people inside and outside recovery circles.

Friendship with Jesus: If you are an agnostic, an atheist, or follow another faith, we hope you will continue to read. We write from the perspective of followers of Christ because that is what we are.

We follow Him because of His gentle and unconditional love.

He is a passionate God who desires intimacy but does not force Himself on anyone.

We are only presenting what we have experienced and what we have seen work for others in pain.

What you decide to do with it is entirely up to you. All we know is - it works!

Richard has been sober and clean, without relapse, for more than forty years.

Dawn has long since stopped enabling and found her voice.

The majority of those we've mentored over the past few decades have successfully stopped using and rebuilt their lives.

We have personally witnessed, time and time again, the miraculous power of the Lord to heal hearts and change lives.

Above all, God's love persuaded us. Genuine love always offers the freedom to receive it or reject it.

Whether people believe in God or not, we always retain the power of choice He gave us.

Religion always tells us what to do. It robs us of the power of choice and renders us powerless.

Friendship with God is different:

2nd Corinthians 3:17 "Where the Spirit of the Lord is, there is liberty."

Where there is liberty, there is also love. And power.

God does not, and will not, make our decisions for us. He gave us the gift of free will; He doesn't want it back. We can turn to Him for guidance, but the power to decide what to do is always ours.

There are times in life when we need more help than other people can provide or that we can give ourselves. Sometimes we need supernatural comfort, counsel, and power to defeat whatever challenge we face.

The moment of decision is such a time.

When we wake up in pain, we need to experience a kind of love more pure, complete, and potent than we humans are capable of on our own.

When we accept Jesus' offer of friendship, we find the love and everything else we need to sustain, heal, and empower us.

We can stop walking in the shallow, powerless existence that led us into addiction and begin to live the full, meaningful, and powerful life we were born to live.

A Mentor. A Real One: A mentor is someone who has been around the barn a few more times than we have, who possesses the character and qualities we would like to acquire for ourselves.

Mentoring often starts as a transactional relationship, with most of the need for help on our side.

Most human relationships are transactional. They are what we call "mutual benefit relationships."

You do something for me, and I do something for you.

Transactional relationships last only as long as they are mutually beneficial.

When the benefit ends, the relationship ends.

There is nothing wrong with this, provided no one is mistreated or manipulated.

Relationships based only on genuine love are rare. There is no mutual benefit involved; we simply love one another. Love-based relationships often require self-sacrifice.

A good friend (we'll call him Joe) suffered a usually fatal heart problem when he was a long way from home. He made it to the hospital alive.

When his best friend heard the news, he immediately jumped on his motorcycle and rode hundreds of miles through the rain, so he could be at Joe's bedside when he woke from his coma.

There was no mutual benefit to riding all that way through rough weather, but there was plenty of love and self-sacrifice.

Love-based relationships are relatively rare. If we have even one, we are blessed.

> Richard: The two most critical mentoring relationships in my life, with Rev. Les Carroll and Apostle Bob Hauselman, grew into genuine, love-based friendships. Our friendships have lasted for decades.
>
> I married Les' daughter. After Jesus, Dawn Marie has been the most important person in my life. Our relationship started as love-based and continues to be love-based.
>
> There are many mutual benefits in our relationship; we help, encourage, and challenge one another. But our marriage is not transactional. Neither of us is keeping score.
>
> Les is still my best friend. When Dawn and I first started dating, he told her it was about time she brought home someone he liked!

Some things are best shared privately with a trusted mentor or close friend, rather than publicly in a recovery group meeting.

Not everyone in recovery is worthy of our trust. We can share whatever is on our hearts with our mentor and be sure our private business won't end up on the street.

A good mentor will avoid making decisions for us. They will not assume a parental role or allow the creation of an unhealthy dependence on them.

They will not rob us of our power of choice. A mentor will encourage and challenge us to make our own decisions.

A good mentor will listen, ask questions, and give us the benefit of their experience.

A wise mentor will not tell us what to do unless they believe we are in imminent danger.

They will offer options, discuss the pros and cons of various courses of action, and ask us what we want to do.

On the day we wake up in our moment of decision, we can call on our mentor for help, even if it is three in the morning.

They will want that call. Our mentor would much rather help us through our crisis than learn later; we died of an overdose.

A wise and experienced mentor will help us uncover and find healing for our unresolved emotional pain.

They will view our behavior, and our overwhelming emotions for what they are, the symptoms of a deep-seated trauma.

They will pray for our healing.

Many Real Friends: If we are serious about recovery and freedom, it is best to stop hanging around with old, substance-abusing friends and find new friends who do not use. Hanging out with our old friends can kill us.

The friends we had when we were using were probably not friends at all.

They may have been people we grew up with, but substance abuse turned them into mere associates, who hung out with us because we had money and dope.

When we got into trouble, they were out of there!

Richard: When I was a prison chaplain, men sometimes told me they missed their old friends. I often asked whether these friends had come to visit them or put money on their books so that they could buy a few commissary items.

The answer was always no.

Case closed.

Coming in from the Cold

Sometimes people abandon us, but we may also isolate ourselves when we are in pain. If we have been in pain our entire lives, being a loner becomes a habit and then a lifestyle.

Loners are outsiders. We keep our business to ourselves. We become observers of life and other people's happiness, rather than participants in life and partakers of life's blessings.

Perhaps when we were young, we were told we were worthless and would not amount to anything - one of the lies that opened the door for the spirit of powerlessness to come in.

Believing this lie strengthens our sense of powerlessness and sets us up for future addictive behavior.

In our loneliness, we may believe no one cares about us—the cords connecting us with other people fray and then break.

Many people may love us, but our broken connectors don't allow us to recognize or receive that love. We sink further into isolation.

We have seen people walk into recovery group meetings or church services where everyone greeted them with warm hugs and asked how they were doing.

Church members had brought them food, given them rides, watched their children, and demonstrated their love in many other ways.

But when we asked if they would like us to pray for them, they told us, "I just don't feel like anyone here loves me."

Pain can blind us to the love others offer us. People with broken connectors cannot connect. They don't know how to connect.. When we don't know how to connect with others, we keep our pain and problems to ourselves.

When tough times come, we bull our way through them without asking for help, until we can no longer bull our way through them. Then we die - or finally, ask for help.

In our broken condition, we carry our lone wolf attitudes and habits with us when we enter recovery. It's what we are used to; it's what we do.

People do what we know to do.

People tell us to ask for help, but we may not know how to ask for help. We are afraid to let our guard down. We are sure if people knew the truth about us, they would reject us.

We are fearful and tired of rejection - of being on the outside looking in. We are frustrated and angry.

We desire acceptance, to belong, but don't know how to come in from the cold.

Friendship with God and having a mentor can help us.

God cracks the doors of isolation and fear open. Our mentor offers us support with skin on it.

Together they encourage us to take risks; to let other people become part of our lives.

Daring to Love

Love is the riskiest business in the universe. It is also beautiful, amazing, and deeply satisfying.

Love makes life worth living; it enables us to live life as fully as possible, whether times are easy or hard.

When we love, we lose our fear.

1st John 4:18 "There is no fear in love; complete love casts out fear."

Love and fear are incompatible, and love is more powerful.

Being with People: Connecting with other people is a key to sobriety and the freedom that can follow.

We were not designed to live in isolation, cut off from all the bonds of friendship.

God created us to be part of a community. He created us to love and be loved.

Love expresses itself through relationships. Friendship with God is the most important one.

Only God knows what is in our hearts. He has the power to heal our brokenness. A mentor helps bring us into relationships with others as we become whole.

"I wish I had friends," we may say. The way to have friends is to be a friend.

We can learn how to be a friend. That is one of the strengths of traditional recovery group meetings. Most people there share a common goal; to get sober and clean and stay that way.

"Ninety meetings in ninety days" isn't only about recovery. It's also about establishing a powerful new habit that brings us in from the cold and gets us around other people.

The more meetings we attend, the more opportunities there will be to meet new people and make new friends.

Finding a Church: Spiritual growth and support are essential if we want to pass through recovery and go on to freedom in Christ.

While we can grow spiritually in a recovery program, we can do even better if recovery groups are not the only places we go for spiritual guidance and growth.

Being part of a community of faith expands our world. It helps us get outside ourselves. We may be needy when we start, but we will also find opportunities to bless others.

It can be hard to walk into a church for the first time. Some are very good at making new people feel welcome; others are not.

In some churches, there isn't much fellowship on Sunday morning. People arrive just before the service starts and leave right after the last "Amen."

In others, you can't get people to stop talking and go home!

Find a church where people don't want to go home.

Perhaps you know someone in your recovery group who goes to a church like that. Why not ask them if you can come along?

To make new friends at church, you can participate in small group meetings, Sunday school classes, Bible studies, and other activities.

You can also ask people to join you for lunch after the Sunday morning worship service.

Richard: When I was single and new to recovery, I joined a church that was very much married couple oriented.

There weren't many single people there. I refused to allow my marital status, or lack thereof, to keep me from taking part in church activities or making friends.

I joined the supper club and ended up in a group with several married couples. Each couple took turns inviting the others to their home for dinner.

When it was my turn to be the host, my guests arrived wondering whether I knew how to cook, and what a single guy was going to serve them.

Dinner went well, except for the whole peppercorns I accidentally put in the salad. Those peppercorns made me famous in the church. I made some excellent friends.

Make the Call: We need friends when we hit our moment of decision. Our mentor may not be available when we need help. If so, the next thing we can do is call our other friends.

When we are in the middle of terrible pain, we should not be alone. Keep calling until someone answers.

Making the call is powerful. Once we make the call, we are 75% of the way to our healing!

Making the call breaks the back of the spirit of powerlessness. It shatters the isolation we may have been living in most of our lives.

Making the call demolishes our pride. It makes us right-sized.

When we are courageous enough to admit we need help, and then reach out to others to get it, our pride goes out the door.

Left unchecked, pride can destroy us and ruin all our hopes.

Some may believe asking for help is a sign of weakness.

Not so. To be blunt, not asking for help is stupid. If you've read this far, we're sure you're not stupid.

2nd Corinthians 12:10b "For when I am weak, then I am strong."

It may seem to be a paradox that asking for help in our weakness makes us stronger - but it does!

When we ask for help, the spirit of powerlessness loses its grip on us.

We become powerful.

Powerful enough to live the life we were born to live.

TREATING OTHERS
AS WE WANT TO BE TREATED

Most of us begin our recovery in a sorry emotional, spiritual, and physical condition. We tend to be selfish and childish. Our tiny world revolves around our needs and wants.

We are generally incapable of genuine, self-sacrificing love.

We may tell our spouse and children we love them. In truth, we love our drug of choice more.

We expect other people to serve us. When they stop giving us what we want, we get rid of them. All our relationships are transactional and disposable.

We're narcissistic and hedonistic. We want to be the center of everyone's attention, and we want to feel good.

We are the only one that matters to us. In our tiny universe, our problems are not molehills quickly dealt with, but mountains of hopelessness we don't know how to climb.

Our problems crowd out the sunlight. They are insurmountable obstacles that occupy much of our attention. We are depressed and powerless.

If we are going to recover, and especially if we seek freedom, our universe must grow larger. Much larger.

How do we expand our world? We grow it when we begin to care about others.

At the start of our recovery, we may have focused on our own needs. To successfully recover and move on into freedom, other people's needs must become important to us as well.

The sooner this happens, the better it will be for all concerned.

Our universe expands when we let other people into our lives. It grows even more when we try to help them.

At some point in your recovery, you will find yourself mentoring someone who is just getting started.

They need the same support and encouragement you needed when you were new. You're just the person to give it to them.[28]

Remember how you felt when you were new in recovery?

Perhaps just a little bit lost? That newcomer may feel the same way.

As we reach out, we would do well to remember to treat other people in the same way we want to be treated.

Let's look at some of the ways we hurt people and what we can do to avoid doing so.

---

[28] Most recovery programs call mentors "sponsors." We prefer to call them "mentors." Sponsors are, by definition, responsible for those they sponsor. We think adults should be responsible for themselves.

Logs and Splinters

Matthew 7:1-5 "Do not judge, so that you will not be judged. For in the way you judge, you will be judged; and by your standard of measure, it will be measured to you.

"Why do you look at the splinter that is in your brother's eye, but do not notice the log that is in your eye? Or how can you say to your brother, 'Let me take the splinter out of your eye,' and behold, the log is in your eye?

"You hypocrite - first take the log out of your eye, and then you will see clearly to take the splinter out of your brother's eye."

We're typically very slow to examine ourselves. Sometimes we altogether refuse to do so. There's a log in our eye, but we are too busy telling others what they're doing wrong to notice it - until we relapse.

We likely relapsed because we did not remove the log from our eye or do the hard work of honest, ruthless, self-examination.

We kept our secrets to ourselves. We did not share our true selves with our mentor, nor did we fully engage with our peers in recovery.

It is much easier to judge others than to examine ourselves.

Judging others is one of the ways we avoid facing our issues.

We continued to be lone wolves, and it hurt us and others. All because we insisted on judging others.

Why do we keep our secrets to ourselves?

Because we are afraid others will judge us!

It's a reasonable fear.

Criticism is Not Constructive

How do you feel when people criticize you? Is it a pleasant experience? Then why do we criticize others?

We find fault with other people under the guise of offering "constructive" criticism.

Criticism, especially when it is unsolicited and delivered in public, is not constructive. It is almost always painful.

Those who habitually find fault with others need healing. They are oblivious to the damage and pain they cause.

To emotionally vulnerable people, criticism, no matter how well-intentioned, feels to them like an attack or assault.

The critic may not intend to hurt anyone, but their motives don't matter. It is how the person who receives the criticism feels that matters.

When we are attacked or believe we're under attack, we tend to respond in one of three ways, none of them productive or helpful:

- ❖ We run away.
- ❖ We defend ourselves.
- ❖ We retaliate.

Running Man: If we run away, we may stay away. We give up on recovery, fearing others will criticize or attack us again. We allow ourselves to be driven away from recovery by someone else's self-righteousness.

Defense: We put up emotional walls to protect ourselves. We reject the possibility there's any merit to the criticism we've received. We harden our hearts.

It may take a long time for someone who raised their defenses in response to criticism to lower them again. Our critique hasn't helped them. It has hurt them and delayed their healing.

Retaliation: Instead of running away or defending ourselves, we strike back at our tormentors.

Many of us are chronically angry to the point of rage, but we are very good at hiding it. The extent of our anger may not reveal itself until it is triggered. One way to unleash someone's hidden fury is to criticize them.

We are angry because we feel powerless. When others criticize us, it feels like they are taking more of our power away.

They are.

We may respond with a laundry list of our critic's faults, expressed at high volume. If we insist on criticizing others, we ought to be prepared to duck and run for cover.

Unsolicited criticism is counter-productive. It may create resentment and damage relationships.

No one likes to be the target of criticism. Where on earth did we get the idea we can criticize others, and they won't mind it?

A Fourth Response: We <u>will</u> be offered "constructive criticism" many times in life. The question is, how will we respond to it?

There is another healthy and potentially healing option. We can <u>listen to criticism</u> from someone who does not have permission to give it. Listening doesn't mean we must agree with it.

159

It will take an effort of the will to listen without getting emotional and defending ourselves, but you can do it! A quick prayer will help.

Let them speak without interruption. When they finish, you can say something along these lines:

"Thank you for your input. I will discuss this conversation with my mentor and consider what you have said."

Then walk away. You have listened politely to your critic's unsolicited input. You do not owe them an explanation or response.

Responding may only prolong the agony. It may also give your critic an undeserved and unearned power over you.

Then talk with your mentor. It's okay to express your anger or other feelings the encounter raised. Just don't do it in front of the person who gave you their input. They don't need to know whether they've hit a sore spot.

If there is any validity to their criticism, your mentor can help you sort it out.

Feedback is Constructive - But Get Permission First

There's a difference between criticism and feedback:

- ❖ Criticism is negative, judgmental, and unsolicited
- ❖ Feedback is positive, affirming, and welcome.

Feedback is useful and valuable. Those who provide it are concerned about our welfare. It provides us with someone else's honest perspective about us. Feedback holds up a mirror, so we can see what we might otherwise miss.

160

Criticism shows us only the negative. Feedback shows us both the positive and the negative.

Feedback does not sting the way criticism does.

Feedback works best when:

> ❖ We enjoy a close relationship with someone that includes our permission to give us honest feedback
>
> ❖ The consent to provide input is mutual
>
> ❖ We understand feedback may sometimes be painful or disturbing
>
> ❖ We know love, and a desire to help us become who we are supposed to be is the motive.

People who are open to receiving potentially painful feedback want to learn, grow, and avoid future pitfalls.

They want help, not judgment.

We can be helpful or judgmental. We cannot be both.

Always Ask First: It is best to ask whether we can share feedback with someone before we share it.

If they tell us no, then we keep our mouths shut.

It's their life, not ours. We do not have permission to interfere.

If they agree to listen, remember - it is best to share hard truths one-on-one, in private. We want to treat other people the same way we'd like to be treated.

Which would you rather receive; judgment or help?

In an Emergency, Break Glass

Proverbs 27:6 "Faithful are the wounds of a friend, but deceitful are the kisses of an enemy."

> Richard: I was a Boston "subway rat" as a kid. I loved to ride the trains. In my day, you could go anywhere on the system for ten cents and a paper transfer.
>
> Sundays after church, my brother and I rode the subway for hours. We took turns standing at the open front window, pretending we were driving the train. The smell of the tunnels still evokes fond memories.
>
> Every car had a lever protected by a pane of glass. Next to it was a small hammer on a chain. The sign above it read, in big red letters: "In an emergency, break the glass." Breaking the glass and pulling the lever would stop the train.

When a friend is in imminent danger, we may not have time to ask for permission before we speak or act. We must stop the train.

It's an emergency. Break the glass. Pull the lever.

Whatever we say may be rejected. It may end a relationship.

But given a choice between putting a friendship on the line and saving someone's life, we will choose to save a life every time.

Gaining lifelong sobriety and freedom is not a game. It is a serious business. In an emergency, it doesn't matter whether people cuss us out at the time or not, provided they stay alive.

If someone has lost a leg and is bleeding out, we're not going to stop to ask permission to apply a tourniquet. We're going to go ahead and do it.

Over decades working with inmates and people with addiction issues, we've witnessed many successes and miracles, as men and women came out of crisis and chaos, passed through recovery, and moved on to freedom and fruitful lives.

We know many people who have succeeded.

But there have also been tragedies along the way, especially deaths from overdose. We know many dead people, too.

> Richard: On at least two occasions, my AA sponsor put our friendship on the line to tell me something I needed to hear.
>
> My initial reaction was anger. The first time, I dropped the f-bomb and left him to pay the check.
>
> Reflection led me to realize he was right. Both times. Today I'm glad he spoke his mind.

We ought to prepare ourselves to hear unsolicited criticism from people who may mean well, but don't know any better. It is going to happen.

It will likely take time, and a degree of healing before we can stop overreacting to criticism.

As we build healthy, positive relationships, we can give those we have come to love permission to provide us with helpful feedback.

Having real friends is a great blessing.

Meanwhile, responses triggered by emotional wounds of the past don't have to drive us away from recovery, freedom, and enjoying healthy relationships.

Shut Up and Listen!

Listening is an acquired skill. We ought to learn to listen.

The cardinal sin in recovery circles is a relapse.

When someone summons the courage to come to a meeting and tell a roomful of potential judges they've relapsed, the best gift we can give them is to shut up and listen.

We owe them the opportunity to share what is on their hearts without interrupting them.

Wouldn't we want the same consideration?

Who among us wants judgment when we need support and encouragement?

We need fewer courtrooms in recovery and more support groups.

People with the courage to share their pain need a chance to get it out on the table, where each person can take a piece and help carry the load.

That can only happen if we shut up and listen.

Listening will not only help our suffering fellow traveler; it will also help us on our journey to wholeness.

We should not be alone on the road. We ought to travel together.

Listening is one of the highest expressions of genuine love there is in this world.

It is also rare. Listening to someone comforts and encourages them. Listening tells them they are valued. It says we care about them.

Listening gets us out of selfishness mode and encourages empathy.

Few people know how to listen. Many in recovery are still too wounded and self-involved to listen to someone else's pain.

In most conversations, we don't listen. We're thinking about what we're going to say when the other person stops talking.

How can we learn to listen? To start:

1. Focus on what the other person is saying.

2. Empty your mind of your agenda.

3. Don't think about what you want to say next while the other person is still speaking.

4. Ask questions related to what they tell you.

5. Repeat some of their statements to ensure you understand. It also lets them know you are paying attention.

When someone gets it that we are listening to them, they will eventually tell us everything, including their deepest secrets.

How do you feel when people don't listen to you?

When no one listens to us, we feel unimportant, insignificant, and powerless.

It is also frustrating, especially when we're on the edge of getting to the heart of something important to us, and we are interrupted.

We must overcome the spirit of powerlessness and the pervasive anger it produces if we are to become addiction free.

Listening to others helps break the back of powerlessness.

When we judge rather than listen to one another, we postpone or even rule out our permanent freedom from addiction.

The best we can hope for is white-knuckled sobriety, and the limbo of tolerable recovery, for the rest of our lives.

We do not have to remain stuck in our misery. We can be free.

Wait for the Rest of the Story

Something that seems very bad at the time it happens, such as a relapse, may produce good fruit in the end.

It is best if we withhold judgment. When we rush to judgment, especially when we pronounce our opinions in harsh black and white terms without room for grace or subtlety, the passage of time may prove us wrong.

The earliest reports and the premature conclusions drawn from them are often wrong, sometimes wildly so.

Just look at our news media. In a rush to be first with a story, they often get it wrong. Retractions are embarrassing.

Life is rarely black or white. The same applies to relapse. There is much to consider before we can begin to understand why it happened. Time may reveal the truth if we are patient enough to wait for it.

Relapse may rob us of hope. We may feel we've messed up. Perhaps we have, but that doesn't mean we're in trouble.

If our relapse didn't kill us, then all it means is we've made a mistake. And we've survived it.

Once we've formed a premature opinion or made a judgment, we tend to stick with it, even in the face of later evidence that reveals we were wrong.

We can be inflexible and unteachable. In a world full of grey areas, inflexibility is a liability. Being unteachable can be fatal.

It takes humility and patience to refrain from judging others and to learn from the experience of others. We will likely need to remind ourselves of the value of humility and work on our pride. Humility and emotional wholeness go hand in hand.

We can always learn something useful from people with more experience in life than we possess. People with years and decades of sobriety under their belts can teach us a great deal, whether we're new to recovery or grizzled old veterans.

We can learn something when others relapse, whether they have years or days' worth of sobriety when it happens. We can also learn from our relapse.

We can learn from people with less life experience than we possess, as well as from those who've been around the barn a few more times than we have. Humility makes it possible.

Relapse doesn't just happen. There's always a reason for it.

If We Do Not Wait Before We Speak

Just as telling other people what to do is counter-productive, so is telling people why <u>we</u> think they relapsed.

We May Be Wrong: We may be rock-bottom positive that we have the answers, but we may be wrong.

We don't always understand our motives; how can we expect to know what's going on in someone else's heart?

They May Not Believe Us: Being right, if we are right, doesn't mean others will believe it. If people think we're wrong, they will reject what we tell them.

Telling someone what is wrong with them and what to do about it may delay or prevent their healing.

It Strengthens Their Sense of Powerlessness: No one likes to be told what to do - especially if they already feel powerless.

To tell someone else what to do is to assume an unwelcome position of authority over them and take away their power.

Their response is more likely to be resentment and anger than agreement with our diagnosis. Unless the idea is theirs, others are unlikely to follow a course of action we recommend.

It Robs People of Their Power: Empowerment is one of the keys to permanent freedom. Unhealthy dependencies prevent freedom. We ought to provide the help that empowers people.

Unfortunately, too much of our charity, our ministry, and what we do in recovery does not empower people. Instead, it fosters unhealthy dependencies.[29]

It's long past time to change that.

Beginning Our Journey to Wholeness

Now we are ready to start our journey through recovery to freedom. The next chapters will introduce the Six Core Principles of the *My Recovery Community.*

---

[29] Read *Toxic Charity,* by Robert D. Lupton. It will change the way you help others.

PRINCIPLE ONE:
YOU ARE NOT POWERLESS!

You are not powerless!

Your life may be chaotic, but <u>only you</u> have the power to decide to overcome your addictive and self-destructive behaviors.

If you ask, God will empower, guide, and strengthen you; but the power of choice is always yours alone.

If a sense or spirit of powerlessness is the emotional root cause of addictive behavior, then the antidote is to empower people to make their own choices.

Recognizing we have been influenced or enslaved by a spirit of powerlessness is the beginning of our empowerment.

Whether we really were powerless or only believed we were powerless, the outcome was the same. We indulged in behavior that helped us numb our pain enough to cope with or entirely ignore our powerlessness.

The same applies to the families of those involved in addictive behaviors. You are not powerless.

You can make choices about how you will live your life, no matter what your addicted family member does.

You can choose to become emotionally whole. You can decide how much and what kind of help you are willing to give the addict in your family, should they choose to stop using.

Only you can decide whether you want to be free. Only you can choose to break the back of your addiction. Only you can choose to take back your power.

We take back our power when we stop being victims, exercise our power of choice, and take responsibility for our decisions and their consequences. With help, we can do this!

No one else can make these choices for you. It is entirely up to you to decide what you want to do.

What Have We Got to Lose?

Rather than help people take back their power, traditional recovery programs require us to "admit we are powerless" over our addictions.

The result: only 5-10% successfully recover.

The idea that twelve-step recovery is the only way to deal with our addictions is deeply ingrained in our society and culture.

It may have been true during much of the 20th century, but it is no longer true today. Today there are other options.

The fear of trying something new may keep us stuck in the rut of failure and defeat. The fear of deviating from "the way we've always done things" makes it harder for people to get free and stay free.

Traditional recovery programs fail for all but a handful of those who turn to them for help. We have absolutely nothing to lose and nothing to fear if we decide to try another way.

The Decision to Use: Bad Idea, But Empowering

How do we know empowerment is the key to a successful, permanent recovery?

We find the answer in the responses to a question we asked hundreds of addicts:

"The last time you used, did you feel 'better' when you used, or when you decided to use?"

The almost universal answer:

"When I made the decision."

Unless we already have the means to get high at hand, there's usually a lag time between the decision to use and our actual relapse. After we decide to use, we must find a drug dealer or get to the liquor store.

Almost everyone we interviewed told us they felt better (empowered) <u>after they decided to use</u>. People did not feel empowered when they used a drug of choice. It was the decision to use that did the job.

The ability to make decisions, even bad ones, restores a sense of having power.

We are powerless to change the decisions made for us without our knowledge or consent. However, we can regain a sense of having power by making smaller, but still significant choices.

The decision to use may appear to empower us. It may feel like empowerment. It is only an illusion. The decision to use is <u>false</u> empowerment.

We may believe we've regained a measure of power or control, but we have not. Deciding to use strengthens the influence of the spirit of powerlessness. It drives us deeper into addiction.

The Traditional Step One Needs a Rewrite

The first of the twelve steps states:

"We admitted we were powerless over our addictions; that our lives had become unmanageable."

As written, this step is a problem. It requires us to subscribe to something that is not true.

We are not powerless. We have the power of choice. We can decide to do something about our addictive behavior, even in the face of an overwhelming desire to use. Choosing to change our lives is powerful!

Once we've made the decision, we can begin to take back our power. We can fight to get our lives back on track.

Admitting we are powerless is not the solution.

Believing we are powerless is the problem.

Powerless? People who use are in trouble because <u>they already feel powerless</u>.

Rather than face and defeat the spirit of powerlessness through empowerment and encouragement, the first step adds to the already unsupportable emotional burden of powerlessness.

It makes the passive acceptance of one's supposed personal powerlessness a prerequisite for recovery.

The first step tells us we do not have the power to conquer our addictions. It requires us to subscribe to the idea our addictions are more powerful than we are.

Time and tradition have firmly planted the idea we are powerless over our addictions in our psyche. It is ingrained in our culture.

Most people in recovery subscribe to this pervasive doctrine without questioning it. We ought to question it.

Powerlessness over our addictions is the foundation of most of today's recovery programs. It is a mantra repeated so often it has assumed the force of law and acquired the gravitas of scientifically-supported fact.

It is neither law nor scientific fact.

The assumption we are powerless over our addictions has helped render traditional recovery programs powerless to prevent all but a few people - only 5-10% - from using.

For the rest, following the traditional first step makes successful long-term recovery harder to achieve.

We are not powerless over our addictions. We have the power to decide to do something about them.

A desire to stop using is enough to get us started. Our journey to wholeness begins when we choose to embrace our power and fight for our lives.

No one recovers alone. We need plenty of help to stop using, but the decision to get sober and clean is a choice only we have the power to make!

We can choose to be powerless, or we can choose to be powerful.

We can remain passive victims who let life and our addictions run us over, or we can become proactive people who make our own decisions and fight to conquer our demons.

Unmanageable? That our lives have become unmanageable is another idea we ought to challenge. It is not always true.

Our lives may be chaotic or may become so, as addiction takes us further down the road to destruction. That doesn't mean our lives are unmanageable.

Many people with addiction issues hold responsible jobs, are financially secure, have healthy family and other relationships, are active in their churches and communities, and enjoy many other blessings and privileges.

They have enough money to purchase their drugs, so they don't steal to feed a habit.

An observer wouldn't know they have an addiction problem.

They may be an emotional mess on the inside, but you wouldn't know it to look at them.

They manage their lives quite well, hiding their secret for years and even decades.

The ability to manage our lives sometimes works against us. It may blind us to the truth that we have an addiction problem.

> Richard: I once stopped drinking for an entire year to win a $50.00 bet and prove I didn't have a problem with alcohol.
>
> One year later, I won that bet, bought a round of drinks for myself and my friends, and picked up right where I had left off.

That I had been able to quit drinking for a year, successfully managing my addiction, allowed me to continue to believe I did not have a problem with alcohol.

At the end of my year of abstinence, I was still a mess on the inside. Spiritually and emotionally, nothing had changed.

Many people subscribe to the notion that "real" addicts lose jobs, relationships, homes, and so on. Not always.

People often compare themselves to gutter drunks and street junkies to maintain the fiction they're not addicted, not one of "those" people.

They point to their ability to manage their lives as evidence they're not hooked.

The ability to manage our lives may help us cling to the illusion we are only "recreational" or "social" users. It may render us unable to assess our condition honestly.

That many addicts manage their lives quite well over time, contradicts the first step's dogmatic assertion of universal unmanageability.

There's no need or reason to wait to get help until we can no longer maintain our relationships, shoulder our responsibilities, or keep up appearances.

We do not have to hit the bottom of losing everything and living on the streets.

We have the power to seek help at any time.

What Does It Mean to "Hit Bottom?"

Lose Everything? Not So Fast: If "hitting bottom" means we must lose everything and land on the streets, then we reject the idea we must hit bottom before we're willing or able to change.

> Richard: A woman I met at an AA meeting in 1980 told me she had had only one drink in her entire life. Just one drink was all it took to persuade her she had a problem with alcohol.
>
> She didn't wait until her life became unmanageable to seek help. She didn't wait to lose her family, friends, business, and everything else she valued.
>
> She acted. She exercised her power of choice. Recognizing she couldn't do it on her own, she got help.
>
> Her life remained manageable. Her decision to get help right away demonstrated she had power over her addiction.
>
> She spared herself and those she loved years of suffering and heartbreak.

Some may think having only one drink doesn't make someone an addict or alcoholic. It's not so much what we use, how much we use, or how often we use that counts.

It's what it does to us and those who love us that matters most.

Hitting Bottom Redefined: Some people lose everything before they are willing to do something about their addiction. That doesn't mean everyone must do the same.

The woman in the above example did not fall very far. She hit her bottom and exercised her power of choice to get help.

Hitting the bottom is often defined as an external condition. It is a belief that addicts must fall until they reach a pre-defined benchmark on a scale of loss, chaos, and pain.

But one size does not fit all. One person's bottom may be another person's top or middle.

That's one of the problems with establishing arbitrary external standards. It is not helpful to create standardized benchmarks for something as personal and subjective as hitting bottom.

Setting up benchmarks gives active addicts an excuse to keep using. They can say, "Compared to so and so, I'm not that bad. I haven't lost everything, so I can't be an addict."

Hitting bottom is not an external condition, but an internal one.

Others may judge by outside appearances, but only addicts know when they have hit bottom.

Only addicts possess the power to decide to stop using and get help.

The Bottom is a Moving Target: We define hitting bottom as someone simply deciding they've had enough.

They realize they needed help, and they get it. How little or how far someone may fall doesn't matter

Whether or not we've hit bottom is self-determined rather than pre-defined by a recovery program - or anyone else.

Only an addict can decide whether they've hit bottom - and are ready to seek help.

The Victimhood Trap

Believing we are powerless and our lives are unmanageable allows us to assume the mantle of victimhood. Our addiction, we claim, is not our fault!

It's easier to blame other people, places, and things for our addictions than to accept responsibility for our choices and their consequences.

Accepting responsibility means we leave our childhood behind, become adults, and get to work to change our stinking thinking and improve our circumstances.

> Richard: The decision to use was my choice, and no one else's.
>
> No one forced me to drink that first beer, smoke that first joint, snort that first crystal, drop that first cap of acid, take my first poke off an opium pipe, or mix that first spoonful of belladonna into a glass of wine and drink it.
>
> I was not a victim - I chose to use. Substance abuse stole fifteen years of my life. The decision I made to stop and get help saved it.

The decision to live or die is entirely yours. What do you want to do?

Tradition is Good – Except When It Isn't

When it comes to winning the war on our addiction, passive resignation to powerlessness gets us nowhere. If it worked, recovery rates would be considerably higher than they are.

Where is the hope in telling people they're powerless over their addictions?

After having the doctrine of personal powerlessness hammered into them at meeting after meeting, how many have abandoned hope they could get free and stay free?

How many have walked out of a recovery program, never to return? How many have died as a result?

After force-feeding us the doctrine of powerlessness, twelve-step recovery tells us our lives have become unmanageable.

To paint everyone with addiction issues with the unmanageable brush is to perpetuate a stereotype; that hitting bottom means losing everything.

Some people's lives may indeed be chaotic, thanks to their addictions. Many addicts have told us they are addicted to chaos.

That doesn't mean our lives are unmanageable. When we get tired enough of our pain, we can decide to climb out of the hole we've dug for ourselves.

Tradition is good when it helps us become whole and free. It connects us to our past and to those who have gone before us.

Tradition makes us aware we are part of something greater than ourselves. It helps us uncover who we are.

Tradition is not good when it enslaves us and closes avenues of potential healing and success.

"We've always done it this way" is the motto of those who only feel powerful when they have power over others. Some people are so frightened of losing control that they will do whatever it takes to prevent change and discourage innovation.

Traditional recovery has its uses. In many ways, it is good. It is just not complete.

We are Not Powerless!

The power to make our own choices is a gift from God. He will not take it back.

Our lives and circumstances may be an utter ruin, but we can still choose to live - or die.

Not even God will make our decisions for us.

We can decide at any time we've had enough. We can decide at any time to do something about our addictive behavior.

Admitting we have a problem may be difficult and painful. It may take time to get there.

It may not happen until staying in our addiction becomes more painful than the pain we are self-medicating

"What do you want to do?"

It is entirely up to you. You are not powerless.

PRINCIPLE TWO:
WE WILL NOT TELL YOU WHAT TO DO

We will not tell you what to do.

The My Recovery Community exists to support and empower you to make your own choices.

We do not judge, blame, or dictate. Instead, we ask: "Have you thought about...?" "What do you think God is saying to you?" And very importantly: "What do _you_ want to do?"

Another issue that surfaced in our conversations with people with addiction issues came in their answers to this question:

"How do you respond when people tell you - you <u>have to</u> do something?"

Here are the top three answers:

"Do the opposite."

"Don't do it."

"Do it because they make me and stop when the pressure is off."

No One Likes to Be Told What to Do

When someone tries to force us to do something, even if doing it would be good for us, our response is often anger, ranging from mild annoyance to unbridled rage. We don't like taking orders.

With anger comes resistance. Whether we openly declare our non-compliance or not, we certainly resist secretly in our hearts.

We comply outwardly, saying what we think people want to hear and doing what we must - but our hearts are not in it.

Real Empowerment

Richard: A few men at the prison where I was the chaplain complained to me about a caseworker who would not send them to a specific halfway house upon their release. He became the target of their anger and frustration.

I asked what was more important to them, feeling better after yelling at the caseworker or going where they wanted to go? They asked me how they could get to the halfway house.

I suggested they apologize for their behavior, tell the caseworker they wanted to make his job easier, wouldn't cause him any more trouble, and were willing to go where he sent them.

They didn't like that advice until I pointed out the man would no longer have any power over them after they left prison. They would have to go where he sent them for a while, but once there, they could apply to transfer to the place they preferred. It would take a bit longer to get there, but wouldn't the extra time and effort be worth it?

They agreed. Rather than sabotage themselves by yelling at the caseworker, the men did as I suggested.

It was their choice. I didn't tell the men what to do. I simply suggested a course of action they could choose to take.

They were empowered and eventually got to go where they wanted to go.

Self-Sabotage is False Empowerment

People sometimes sabotage themselves rather than submit to authority.

The decision to resist authority may seem like empowerment, but all we usually accomplish is a further loss of power. We only make ourselves miserable, and our lives more difficult.

Welcome to D Block: A prison in the northeast has a special cellblock; a prison within the prison to house their most hardened inmates; men who would rather die than comply.

The men in D Block had proven to the prison system they were tough guys. The state agreed they were tough, took away most of their privileges, and locked them up where flies don't land.

The men stay in a one-person cell for twenty-three and a half hours a day. They are only allowed out for half an hour to exercise by themselves in an outdoor cage.

The men are allowed only one or two showers a week. They eat all their meals in their cells, delivered through a hatch in their cell door. A dirty little plexiglass window in the door allows them a restricted view of the block.

The shouting, cursing, and banging on the doors is deafening. The stench of human waste, rotting food, and unwashed bodies is so foul it is almost visible, like a mist hanging in the air.

Anger, Pride, and Powerlessness: Some of these men were found guilty of serious crimes, but most were guilty of relatively minor offenses.

It wasn't the severity of their crime that landed them in D Block; it was their bad behavior after they got to prison.

Deciding whether to behave themselves is one of the few choices prisoners can make. Behaving would have made their lives easier.

They might have served their time in the relative freedom of a general population dormitory. But the men in D Block rejected the more comfortable way.

They sabotaged themselves.

All they had to do was obey the rules and follow orders. Had they done so, they might also have earned an early release. It would have been in their best interest to be model prisoners, but they opted for non-cooperation and violence.

Some may say they were too proud to cooperate. If so, it was pride driven by a sense of powerlessness.

These men resisted authority in a futile attempt to retain or gain power. Their resistance led to the loss of what little power they still possessed.

Doing time isn't easy, but it could have been easier. Choosing to behave would have been a rational decision.

These men were not rational. Their powerlessness and rage, aggravated by their loss of freedom, overruled rational thought.

Non-compliance made them feel powerful but did not make them powerful. It was counterfeit empowerment. Self-sabotage led to a further loss of power.

The spirit of powerlessness can so enslave and blind us that we will go to any length to regain a sense of having power, even to the extent of causing ourselves additional, avoidable suffering.

These men won nothing except bragging rights with their equally powerless neighbors locked in the other D-block cells.

For them, the illusion of having power was more important than having actual power and enjoying a more comfortable life.

Compliance is Not Enough

Being forced to do something is unlikely to produce good long-term results. Our hearts will not be in it. The moment the pressure is off, we will resume doing whatever we want to do.

Forced compliance only cleans the outside of the cup. Our behavior is the only thing that changes. Meanwhile, the inside of the cup - our heart - remains untouched.

If we are going to become truly free, we must clean the inside of our cup. If it is not clean, the outside will become dirty again.

We will relapse.

The decision to change our heart is a choice only we can make.

No one else can make it for us, though some will try. Our choice must be made freely, without pressure. Coercion only produces reluctant outward obedience - and inner rebellion.

It doesn't produce lasting good fruit.

That is why we don't tell people what to do. We conquer the spirit of powerlessness, and our addictive behavior, by taking back the power to make our own choices.

A positive change of <u>behavior</u> leads to recovery, though our recovery may not last for long. Most people relapse.

A positive change of <u>heart</u> leads to permanent freedom. We can decide to go for it, but only God can do it. He will not do it against our will.

If we change our minds, God will change our hearts. He will not force us to decide one way or the other.

A Change of Behavior Has Value: Changing only our behavior is not enough, but it has value. It offers the short-term benefit of not using.

While it is better not to use than to use, changing only our behavior is not complete. It falls far short of our goal of permanent freedom.

If all we have done is change our behavior without changing our hearts, then any positive change will not last - especially if we were forced to change it.

Forced Submission Doesn't Work: Being forced to do things often produces the opposite of the desired outcome.

Why? Because we don't like to be told what to do. We resist when others boss us around, put us in a subordinate position, or treat us like children.

People who habitually dominate others are battling against <u>their</u> sense of powerlessness. They need healing. The only path control freaks see to becoming powerful is to control the people and the environment around them.

The use of power to bend others to our will is destructive. It is a cry for help.

Truly powerful people, who walk in love and freedom, have no such desire for power over others. They have nothing to prove to anyone. Their power comes from within.

Being forced to submit to another's will robs us of our God-given right to make our own choices. It takes away our power.

How do we respond to coercion? We may comply outwardly, pretending to submit. We may refuse to submit, or do the opposite of what someone tells us to do.

If people want to force us to stay sober and clean, we'll refuse to do it. How convenient.

Our Way or the Highway

The idea their way is the only way renders twelve-step recovery ineffective as a means of achieving long-term sobriety. It may not be any program's official position, but it is undoubtedly a prevailing attitude in many recovery circles.

They would have us believe we have no other choice but to do it their way. It is an outdated belief with roots in the days when twelve-step recovery was the only game in town.

For much of the twentieth century, it was "our way or the highway."

Think about it. If your life and sobriety depended on working, the only program there was, what happens to you if it doesn't work?

What happens if you relapse? Where else can you go for help?

No wonder people were fearful. For many years there was no other place to go for help - but this is no longer true.

Today there are many alternatives to twelve-step recovery. The days of "our way or the highway" are over.

Twelve-step recovery is still the best known and most utilized option, but it is no longer the only game in town.

Pick your road. It's your choice.

Self-Appointed Judges

Too many people judge others, blame others, and tell others what to do. That may be how the world functions, but shame, judgment, and blame have no place in recovery.

Some self-appointed finger-pointers are new to recovery and simply do not know any better. Others have been around for a while and ought to know better.

Some old-timers seem to think their length of sobriety gives them a license to judge others and tell them what to do. It doesn't.

Silence Really Can Be Golden: Most of us would be better off to listen more and speak a whole lot less.

It would help everyone if, rather than tell others what they did wrong and what to do, we limited our speaking to sharing our testimonies, our struggles, defeats, lessons learned, and victories.

Others may find our experiences helpful - but telling others what to do is often not helpful at all.

Judging others, highlighting their faults and failures, and then telling them what they should have done, is arrogant and presumptuous.

When we do it in an open meeting instead of in private, it is insensitive, embarrassing, and rude.

It is also self-centered. We are so focused on laying our "wisdom" on people who usually haven't asked for it, and so in love with the sound of our voice, that we don't stop to consider the other person's circumstances or feelings before we speak.

It is easier to find fault with others, blame others, and judge others than it is to examine ourselves.

People who habitually judge others and tell them what to do are often running from their pain.

What if We Listened?

Listening is far more powerful, useful, and healing than talking.

It is also rare.

Listening is one of the most potent expressions of genuine love there is in this world.

Listening to someone, especially someone in pain, validates them.

Listening makes people feel loved and valued. It tells them they are not alone in their struggles. Listening encourages people; it gives them strength and hope.

Many people use because no one listened to them. Many drop out of recovery because people in group meetings, consumed by their problems, don't listen to other people when they express their pain.

When people try to share what's on their hearts, other people sometimes shut them down. They interrupt them, judge them, and give them unsolicited advice.

Proverbs 18:13 "He who gives an answer before he listens, it is folly and shame to him."

We would all be better off if we took care of our own business.

Can we agree to do more listening and less judging and telling other people what to do?

Is attendance at your recovery group dwindling? It may be because group members don't listen enough and tell people what to do too often.

Encourage in Public, Challenge in Private

After suffering public judgment and embarrassment, how many people have walked away from recovery, never to return? How many have died as a result?

Proverbs 27:6 "Faithful are the wounds of a friend, but deceitful are the kisses of an enemy."

R-E-S-P-E-C-T: Respect for the privacy of others goes a long way toward building solid relationships. But sometimes, it is necessary to challenge a friend's attitudes or behavior when we believe they are in imminent danger of relapse.

We have no business judging others, but radical changes in behavior can indicate someone we care about is in trouble.

A true friend will ask what's going on and offer help.

Our fears may be way off base. We may believe someone is in trouble and bring it to their attention, only to find we are wrong.

That is why it is best to encourage in public but challenge in private. It is respectful and avoids embarrassment. Our friend will not be embarrassed if we are right, and we will avoid embarrassment if we are wrong.

It is better to be wrong and apologize than to let someone we care about fall off a cliff. Love tells the truth, even when it hurts.

Buy-In versus Push-Back

When people asked us how to get out of prison and stay out, or how to get off drugs and stay off, we used to give them a laundry list of things we wanted them to do.

We didn't understand why some of them didn't stick around, though they seemed very motivated to succeed.

People don't like being told what to do. We were telling them what to do. Our motives were good, but our methods were not.

The spirit of powerlessness robs people of their power. When we told people what to do, we took away more of their power.

We changed the way we mentored people. We stopped telling them what to do.

We're not perfect. Not by a long shot. But today we try to do more listening to people than talking at them. By listening, we learned a great deal about them, including how we might help them.

By asking people what they wanted to do, we empowered them. We started to get more buy-in and a lot less push-back.

People still ask us how to get out of prison and stay out and how to get off drugs and stay off. These days, we don't tell them what to do. We listen and ask questions.

Over time we get to know one another. We have conversations rather than give lectures. As a good friend is fond of saying, we've learned to "scratch people where they itch."

What Do <u>You</u> Want to Do?"

We no longer tell people what to do.

Instead, we ask, "What do <u>you</u> want to do?"

Asking people what <u>they</u> want to do empowers them to take charge of their recovery. It is their choice, and no one else's as it should be.

When someone makes a decision, they own it - and are far more likely to follow through.

We repeat: when people answer the "What do you want to do" question, they assume responsibility for their recovery.

Their recovery is no longer a program or a person telling them what to do. Whatever they decide to do is <u>their</u> idea.

If someone decides to stop using, then they can be shown options. We can then discuss the potential benefits and pitfalls of each one.

It is then up to them to decide what road to take on their journey to wholeness.

When mentors tell addicts what to do, and it doesn't work out, addicts can blame their mentors for the failure, whether they took the recommended action or not.

But when a course of action is an addict's choice, they cannot blame someone else for steering them wrong if they fail to follow through, or if they hit a rough patch in the road.

When it's our choice, we own it. The blame game no longer works.

My AA Sponsor Never Told Me What to Do

Richard: "David" was a quiet, peaceful man, with more than twenty years of unbroken sobriety, when I met him in 1980.

He didn't speak much in meetings, but when he did, people paid attention. He had wisdom, serenity, and enjoyed life.

He was a great listener.

They told me to find a sponsor who had what I wanted and hang out with him to learn how he got it. I wanted what David had. He agreed to be my sponsor.

I'm sure I drove him crazy, but he never complained. He was patient. Sometimes we'd grab a cup of coffee after a meeting and talk. Well, I spoke. He mostly listened.

I cannot recall him ever telling me what to do. But I still remember the questions he asked.

One time, he asked me when I was going to grow up.

At twenty-eight, I thought I was an adult, but my language reflected my immaturity. Let's just say the "f-bomb" was a prominent part of my vocabulary.

I didn't realize my language revealed the condition of my heart.

David told me mature adults didn't use gutter language. He asked me again when I was going to grow up.

That made me angry. I dropped the f-bomb on him as I left. But his question wouldn't go away.

I thought everyone cursed the way I did. But then it dawned on me; I had never heard David use foul language.

That opened my eyes. Everyone did not curse, especially people who possessed the strength and serenity I coveted.

I decided to stop cursing. It was hard, and it took time, but I eventually succeeded. That's not to say an offensive word doesn't slip past my lips now and then, but the stream of filth that used to pour forth whenever I opened my mouth has dried up.

Another day, I was complaining about my girlfriend's previous lover. He occasionally called to cuss her out. If I was home, I took the phone from her and cussed him right back - stupid, obscenity-laced, macho stuff.

He always hung up before I could get all my licks in. Every call left me angry and frustrated.

After listening to me rant about his most recent call, David asked me how I liked being "owned by that guy." I asked David what he meant.

David pointed out I was allowing this guy to ruin my day, even lying awake at night thinking about revenge.

My sponsor promised me my enemy was sleeping soundly, not even thinking about me. He asked me again how I liked being owned by this guy.

I didn't like it. It hadn't occurred to me that my enemy owned me.

I asked David what to do about it. He told me to be kind to him the next time he called.

A few weeks later, he called again. Somehow, I managed to be kind to him. This time he was the one all stirred up when he hung up.

Months passed before he called again. He was calm and quiet. We had a brief, polite conversation, said goodbye, and hung up. The war was over. We weren't friends, but we were no longer enemies. And he didn't own me anymore.

David challenged me but never told me what to do. He listened, asked questions, made suggestions, and warned me about traps to avoid.

My sponsor earned the right to advise me but never tried to run my life. He challenged me to leave boyhood behind and become a man. He was a friend, a role model I tried to emulate.

The Lord brought David into my life. I will never forget him.

What Do Family Members Want to Do?

Dawn: One of the mistakes I made when trying to help enablers was to tell them they had to give up a destructive relationship with an abusive man.

All I accomplished was to force the women I was trying to help to choose between me and "the man they loved." The women would either stop coming to our meetings or simply start lying to me. They also coached their kids to lie.

By backing them into a corner, I robbed them of their power and damaged our relationship. Once trust is lost, it takes a great deal of effort and time to regain it.

Tough Love is Not Always Loving: Another relationship breaker is to tell parents not to help their addicted adult children. It goes against every fiber of their being.

If they are willing to let us, we can teach parents how to help their children without enabling further destructive behavior.

It's not enough to restore addicts' power of choice. Family members need to have their power restored as well.

Family members must be able to decide, without coercion, what kind of help they are willing to receive - or provide.

Each family member must have the power to decide whether they will stay in a relationship with an addict or end it and get away from the chaos.

Adults may make the most important decisions for them. Still, the children of addicts need an age-appropriate degree of decision-making power if they are to avoid becoming addicts, too.

Given the right kind of help, the children of inmates and addicts can choose positive role models, discover their gifts and talents, and create for themselves a fulfilling and prosperous future.

Whether an addict or a member of the addict's family, we need more than a change of behavior. We need a change of heart.

We cannot change our hearts. God will not change our minds.

But if we change our minds, God will change our hearts!

PRINCIPLE THREE:
NO ONE RECOVERS ALONE

No one recovers alone.

Recovery should not be centered on the addict alone.

Since family members, friends, and the community are all affected by an addict's attitudes and behavior, all need to recover. Recovery works best when we recover together.

As difficult as it may be for actively-using addicts to admit they have a problem, it can be even more difficult for members of an addict's family to admit they also have a problem.

Many of us resist the idea we need help. We think asking for help is a sign of weakness. We do not want anyone to think we are weak.

But asking for help is not a sign of weakness, but a sign of strength. We are just not accustomed to the idea that reaching out for help makes us stronger.

What happens to the lone wolf? It dies.

Wolves live in packs; it is unnatural for a wolf to live alone. A lone wolf must do everything itself if it means to survive. But in a pack, the burden is shared.

Genesis 2:18 "It is not good for the man to be alone."

It is the same with human beings. We need to live in family and community.

While many people are happy and comfortable to be single, many others prefer to share their lives with that one particular person in a covenant of marriage. Single or married, our need for family and community is fundamental.

Being part of a community brings many benefits. Living in a community adjusts our attitudes and hones our world view. We can learn from others how they succeeded in areas where we struggle.

We can learn from the wisdom and experience of others. We can share our experiences and our insights to assist others. We can find joy and comfort in simply being together. We can learn how to resolve conflict and make room for every person to become who they were born to be.

We can uncover what we are still missing and recognize where we need healing. We can also gain a family. One of the results of addiction can be the loss of our extended family.

In a community, we find the support and strength we need when times are tough, and our recovery and freedom are at risk. We share our joys, heartaches, triumphs, and struggles.

Recovery works best when all recover together. Together, we can share the power of love and freedom. We can support one another, helping one another stand back up and keep going if we fall. When a family recovers together, no one is left behind.

PRINCIPLE FOUR:
RELAPSE DOESN'T MEAN
WE START OVER

Relapse doesn't mean we start over.

Whether days, weeks, or years, the time we remained abstinent, clean, and sober still counts. It is a foundation of success we can build on.

All experience is useful if we learn from it.

Relapse reveals where we need further growth and healing.

In traditional recovery circles, relapse is almost the worst thing that can happen to us. It doesn't have to be.

A relapse may not be pretty, but if we are willing, we can learn from it. We can gain strength. We can defeat the spirit of powerlessness.

Becoming Right-Sized

We keep score in life to determine how well we're doing.

Are we winning? Are we losing? Are we doing better than our friends and neighbors?

Are we richer, smarter, more attractive, more spiritual than others?

Knowing how well we're doing at any given time can be useful, provided we avoid becoming prideful about it.

There's a difference between having a healthy appreciation for ourselves and our gifts and thinking too highly of ourselves.

When channeled into doing good for others as well as for ourselves, ambition is good. It becomes destructive when we run over and hurt other people to get what we want.

Let us become right-sized, neither too big, nor too small.

1ˢᵗ Thessalonians 4:11a "Make it your ambition to lead a quiet life; attend to your own business, and work with your hands."

Tracking our progress as we recover can be useful, provided we avoid being too hard on ourselves when things go wrong.

It's normal to feel discouraged after a relapse, but with help, we can uncover what triggered it and then act to fix it.

We don't want to let a setback send us into depression or make us believe we have failed. We want to keep on doing the right thing for ourselves.

We can avoid becoming mired in self-pity and paralysis. We can embrace positive change.

We can stop running away from what ails us, begin to stand tall, and conquer.

All experience, whether good or bad, can be useful if we learn from it. We can learn a great deal from relapse.

We can also avoid future relapse if we apply what we learn.

If We Relapse

Many recovery programs hand out plastic or metal tokens to recognize the attainment of various lengths of sobriety. It's encouraging to get one. A sobriety chip means success.

But sometimes we fail. We don't want to relapse until the day we do. Our circumstances and emotions overwhelm us. We use to escape them.

Remaining clean and sober for a lifetime without relapse is the goal, but in twelve-step recovery, only a few people manage it.

It may help take away some of the sting of a temporary "slip" if we remember relapse is, for most people, a normal part of the recovery process.

Relapse most often feels like a setback, the most discouraging, and potentially dangerous occurrence in recovery - but relapse does not have to be an entirely negative experience.

We can turn it into something useful and powerful if we are willing to learn from it.

Relapse reveals where we still need healing. That's an excellent thing! With the help of God, our mentor, and other trusted friends, we can uncover the reasons we relapsed.

Relapse can provide us with a path forward to deal with the spiritual, emotional, and other issues it reveals. Treating a relapse as a learning opportunity can bring us closer to permanent freedom from addiction.

The Time We Were Sober and Clean Still Counts

In traditional recovery circles, relapse is a negative experience we must avoid at all costs. They are right about avoiding it if we can.

If we relapse, the self-appointed finger-pointers and experts in our recovery group will spring into action. They will tell us what we did wrong, often without bothering to ask us what happened.

If they remember to ask before they speak, they are likely to consider anything we tell them as an excuse to justify our using, rather than a sincere attempt to figure out what happened, and why.

They may tell us to go back to the beginning and start over.

They will tell us the program did not fail to work - we failed to work the program.

The program is always right. Relapse is our fault, or so our judges say.

After judgment comes sentencing. We may become an object of horror, an example of what happens to someone who doesn't fully work the program.

They may demote us to second-class membership in our recovery group. We may be told not to speak, but to shut up and listen.

It's no wonder people often keep a relapse to themselves or stop coming to meetings altogether. Very few are brave enough to endure the pain and embarrassment of public humiliation.

Most people in recovery relapse at least once. That ought to be a good reason to refrain from judging people who struggle with their sobriety.

Some people do not consider the impact of their words before they speak. The "advice" they give may be entirely off the mark, and hurtful.

A Relapse is Not a Failure: A relapse is undoubtedly a negative experience if it kills us, but if we survive it, it can be positive and beneficial.

We're not advocating that anyone relapse on purpose because it <u>might</u> be beneficial for them. Grasping at any cockamamie excuse to use, no matter how ridiculous or far-fetched, is part of our old stinking thinking.

If you've relapsed, take heart. If you're breathing, your heart is beating, and you can read what we're writing, then <u>you did not fail</u>.

The program failed. The program failed you.

It failed you because it does not address the emotional root cause of addiction, a sense or spirit of powerlessness.

People who relapse do not need judgment. They need hope, restoration, and healing.

Stay the course. You don't have to let criticism and judgment keep you from moving on in your journey to wholeness.

Stick with people who encourage and support you. Your real friends will challenge you but will not judge you. They will help you figure out what went wrong and help you get up and get going again.

We do not judge or humiliate anyone for relapsing, or any other reason. Remember, more people in recovery relapse than do not.

With the risk of relapse as high as it is, no one in recovery who dares to judge others has a leg to stand on.

1st *Corinthians 10:12 "Let him who thinks he stands to take heed he does not fall."*

An eagerness to judge others is a sign of arrogance. Arrogance leads to relapse. If they relapse, those who judged you will not enjoy their own time in the hot seat.

Sometimes what goes around really does come around.

In the *My Recovery Community*, relapse doesn't mean we turn in our sobriety tokens and start over at the beginning. Whether six days or six years, the time we were sober and clean still counts. It's a track record of success we can build on.

Fear is Normal: The judgment and condemnation we may receive from our family and peers are motivated to a high degree by their fear.

If we relapse, family members who may have come to believe our recovery was going to last, begin to fear "everything" is about to start all over again.

They may be discouraged at the return of old behavior. Our family members are waiting for the circus to resume, bracing themselves for more disappointment and pain.

The relapse of a recovery group member reminds everyone they are vulnerable, especially if the one who relapsed was a sponsor, an old-timer, or someone who seemed to have it all together. The relapse of someone close to us can be shocking.

Recovery is a journey. There are going to be potholes in the road. Relapse is often part of the trip. All we can do is keep doing what we have the power to do.

Can we listen without judging? Can we support without enabling? Can we guide without dictating? Can we seek our growth and healing no matter what choices others make for themselves?

If an addict relapses, family members need to avoid joining them in relapse. We want to prevent a return to the days when the addicted family member, and the chaos they created, took all the family's attention and drained people of their energy, hope, and resources.

Family members can keep their peace and sanity, even if an addict they love continues to self-destruct.

Each of us is supposed to be responsible for our own lives, the decisions we make, and the consequences of our choices.

We always have the freedom to run away from our pain, but running away almost always leads to more pain.

Rather than allow a relapse to become a permanent monument to failure, we can turn it into something useful and powerful.

We can let it destroy us, or we can learn from it on our way to a fuller, freer life.

Options After Relapse

Assume for the moment you've relapsed. Now, what do you want to do about it? Whether you are an addict or a member of an addict's family, you have three choices:

- ❖ You can give up on yourself and remain powerless.

- ❖ You can pretend it didn't happen and keep it a secret.

- ❖ You can learn from the experience and keep growing.

Before you decide what to do, you should know choosing one of the first two options will not help you, and very likely will cause you further harm. Only the third option will help you grow and live.

Taking the Easy Way Out: Giving up and remaining powerless, or pretending it didn't happen and keeping our relapse a secret, may seem to be the most comfortable choices.

But isn't choosing the easy way out part of our problem?

Given a choice between doing what seemed easiest at the time, and doing what may be more difficult and painful, but right, how often have we chosen the easy way out? Isn't that what we've always done? And where has taking the easy road led us?

It may seem easier to pick up our poison of choice to dull and avoid our pain, but in the long run, it makes things worse. Pain always catches up with us until we finally deal with it.

The quick fix is no fix at all. It either delays the inevitable or brings us more quickly to destruction. It is not easy to face our pain, deal with it, and become free. Most people choose the easy way. They don't make it.

Matthew 7:13-14 "Enter through the narrow gate; for the gate is wide and the way is broad that leads to destruction, and there are many who enter through it.

"For the gate is small and the way is narrow that leads to life, and there are few who find it."

Every time we decide to take the easy way and use, we dig our hole a little deeper until we dig our own grave. One final relapse topples us into it. That's the story for too many of us.

Do the Hardest Thing First: If we do the hardest thing first, everything else we do will be easier!

For many people, the hardest thing to do was swallow our pride and admit we have an addiction problem. The next hardest thing was to do something about it.

It will take time before it gets easier, but if you stay the course, learn from others and make more good choices than bad ones, life will be better – even when it's hard!

If we want to get out of the hole we've dug, the first thing to do is – stop digging!

No one in recovery wants to relapse, but the fact is, more people relapse than achieve long-term or life-long sobriety.

Only one person in one hundred who have struggled with addiction will die sober, clean, and without ever relapsing.

Don't let this discourage you. This book and the *My Recovery Community* based on it offers you an opportunity not only to recover but to become free and whole.

We can do better, much better. We can live and not die. We can live the life we were born to live, rather than settle for so much less.

Yes, relapse can set us back. It can get us thrown out of a halfway house we fought to get into. It may violate the terms of our release and send us back to jail or prison.

It can be the last straw with family and friends who finally lose hope and patience, and decide they want nothing more to do with us.

Relapse can also be dangerous. There is no guarantee we will survive the next time we use.

Anything can happen; an overdose, a fatal auto accident, or being shot and killed because we were in the wrong place at the wrong time.

But relapse can also be useful. We can learn from it. Relapse reveals areas where we still need healing.

It's the End of the World as We Know It

Relapse can kill us. That would be the end of this world for us.

We ought to do whatever we can to avoid it. But if we survive it, relapse can bring healing. If we pursue our healing instead of giving in to despair, relapse can lead to spiritual, emotional, and behavioral breakthroughs.

It can lead us out of the world of death we have been living in and into a new world, an addiction-free world! That would be the end of the world as we knew it and the start of a new one.

And we would feel fine!

If we should not tell people why we think they relapsed and what to do to prevent a recurrence, then what should we do?

We're about to find out.

PRINCIPLE FIVE:
PERMANENT FREEDOM
FROM ADDICTION IS POSSIBLE

Permanent freedom from addiction is not only possible; it is God's desire.

God works in us to bring about spiritual rebirth, cognitive regeneration, the healing restoration of our souls, and the development of mature spiritual fruit.

Recovery or Freedom?

Recovery and freedom are not the same. In recovery, we stop using. In freedom, the issues driving our addictive behavior have been addressed and are no longer a factor.

As we stated earlier, we believe it is possible to recover without the help of a higher power; but when we talk about freedom, we are talking about freedom in Christ.

Recovery is good, but it is not complete. Freedom is complete.

Whether you choose a lifetime in recovery or a lifetime of freedom is entirely up to you.

Freedom!

How does permanent freedom from addiction look?

Here are a few benchmarks:

❖ We face and deal with painful emotions, tough times, and severe life issues without resorting to alcohol, drugs, and other damaging addictive behaviors.

❖ We live in the present moment.

❖ Past traumas lose their power over us.

❖ We no longer fear the future.

❖ We cease to be outcasts, outsiders, or loners. We may be introverts, but we participate fully in life.

❖ We have accepted Jesus' offer of friendship and enjoy a moment-to-moment relationship with Him that goes well beyond powerless, legalistic, religious observance.

❖ We enjoy healthy, God-pleasing relationships.

❖ We walk in love, freely receiving it and giving it away.

❖ We are concerned about the welfare of others and act on our concerns.

❖ We exhibit the fruit of the Holy Spirit.

❖ We are powerful but do not misuse or abuse our power.

We can remain in recovery for a lifetime and enjoy at least some of the blessings and benefits of freedom, but if we go on to freedom, we can get them all!

White-Knuckled Sobriety

White-knuckled sobriety aptly describes the emotional condition of many people in recovery. It means we much fear relapse.

We hold on to sobriety so tightly our knuckles become white with the effort. Maintaining white-knuckled sobriety is an awful lot of work. It is certainly not freedom.

Some call it a "dry drunk." We're not using, but inside we still think and feel as if we were using. We are spiritually and emotionally stuck.

There is a season for white-knuckled sobriety. It only becomes an issue if we get stuck in it long-term.

To live with white knuckles is not living. It is survival. Our destiny is freedom.

Freedom begins when we lose the fear of relapse. When we no longer fear, we stop living like addicts, stop settling for tolerable recovery, and start to live like free human beings.

Most of us do not get to freedom; we live instead in tolerable recovery.

We're not using, but we have at least learned to live with our pain. That's fine if we're satisfied with it.

Tolerable recovery is good; it means we've made progress. We have gained the ability to function.

We are not using, but we're probably still a mess on the inside.

Freedom is complete. When freedom comes, fear, including the fear of relapse, evaporates.

A Little Fear is Not a Bad Thing

There is no guarantee we will survive the next time we use; a little fear in the early days of our recovery is not a bad thing.

The problem begins when we get stuck in fear.

For those who seek permanent freedom, a passing season of white-knuckled sobriety is a normal part of the healing process.

The fear of relapse during the early days of our recovery helps keep us awake and alert. It helps us avoid complacency and taking foolish risks.

In the beginning, fear of relapse may help us make the right decisions, such as staying away from people who are likely to pressure us into using and avoiding places and situations where we are likely to be trapped and tempted.

One size does not fit all. There is no template for how long the white-knuckled season should last.

Each person heals in different ways and at different rates; some heal quickly, others over time.

White-knuckled sobriety is a barrier to recovery and freedom only if it becomes a permanent rather than a temporary state.

Whether we move on from tolerable recovery to permanent freedom is a choice that is always up to us.

Only we can decide what we want to do.

Don't Feed the Sacred Cows

There are many sacred cows in traditional recovery circles.

Two especially get in the way of our becoming whole and free:

- ❖ Addiction is a disease.
- ❖ Once an addict, always an addict.

Our fifth core principle - that permanent freedom is possible - rejects both assumptions.

While people are not required to agree with us to be part of the *My Recovery Community,* they will likely find it difficult to become free while continuing to feed these sacred cows.

Sacred Cow #1 - Addiction is a Disease: To stay focused on our primary goal of addressing the emotional root cause of addictive behavior and helping people break free of addiction, we are not going to discuss the disease theory at length.[30]

That addiction is a disease is a matter of faith for many. We don't want to argue with anyone about it.

Arguments over matters of faith are rarely fruitful. If believing it's a disease helps people recover, that's great.

> Richard: I believed addiction was a disease during the early years of my recovery. That is what they told me when I first joined the program.
>
> My first taste of freedom changed my thinking.

---

[30] Many books have been published on the subject. No doubt you can find them online.

We base our conviction that addiction is a behavior on:

- ❖ Research shedding new light on the nature of addiction.
- ❖ The low success rates (5-10%) for recovery programs based on the disease theory.
- ❖ Richard's experience as a former substance-abuser.
- ❖ Dawn's experience as a former enabler.
- ❖ Decades helping others begin their successful journeys to wholeness.

<u>If addiction is a disease, then it is the only disease people without medical or mental health training are permitted to treat.</u>

Challenging the assumptions traditional recovery is based on is healthy. Only good can result from ongoing research and adult conversations about the findings.

Addiction is not a disease. It is a behavior that can be changed, provided the root cause of the behavior, a sense or spirit of powerlessness, is appropriately addressed.

When we pull up the root, the plant dies. It is the same with addictive behavior.

Sacred Cow #2 - Once an Addict, Always an Addict: Addiction is hard to beat, but beat it we can! Addictive behavior does not have to be a life-long scourge.

The "always an addict" doctrine denies the possibility of anyone ever becoming whole and free. It means the best we can hope for is the limbo of tolerable recovery.

It means we are still in emotional pain, but we have learned how to live with it without using. It means the fear of relapse will always be with us, even if only in the background.

It also means we wear a permanent, invisible sign that labels us as addicts to ourselves and others.

"My name is _____, and I'm an addict."

Tradition requires us to introduce ourselves this way whenever we speak at a twelve-step recovery group meeting.

Heaven help us if we only state our name, have the audacity to say we've recovered, or - horrors - tell people we have been set free and are no longer addicts.

Continuing to say we're an addict or an alcoholic becomes more than a phrase we repeat so that no one will be upset with us.

Repetition may reinforce the notion that being an addict is who we are. To continue to label ourselves as an addict makes addiction part of our identity. It defines us as human beings.

Once being an addict becomes an ingrained part of our identity, it is hard to shake; but shake it, we must, if we want to be free.

Other people are going to judge and reject us, call us addicts, and put us in one of their neat little file folders. In their eyes, our addictions define us and guide how they relate to us.

That being the case, why should we do the same thing to ourselves?

Other people may put us in a pigeonhole, but we do not have to cooperate with them!

Frequently confessing we're addicts doesn't liberate us. It implies we can never be free. There is neither hope nor a future in it.

Yes, it is important to acknowledge we have a problem; but the point of admitting it is to solve it, not to wallow in powerlessness for the rest of our lives.

If we want to live in freedom, we must stop giving self-pity a foothold, stop being victims, and become responsible - and powerful - adults!

Our addictions do not define us. They are not who or what we are.

Using is something we do (or did). It is a behavior that can change.

If we change our behavior for long enough, we can then address the underlying spirit of powerlessness driving our addictions.

As we deal with our powerlessness, our hearts will begin to heal until we are free.

The disease theory of addiction and the idea we are doomed to remain addicts for the rest of our lives are incompatible with what the *My Recovery Community* stands for.

We believe full freedom is not only possible; it is God's desire.

Tolerable Recovery Means Settling for Less

Ideally, tolerable recovery is a season or process we pass through on our way to freedom. It is good, but not complete.

When Jesus healed the blind, He healed both eyes. When He healed the lepers, He healed their entire bodies.

When Jesus healed the paralyzed man, He didn't tell him to pick up his mat and limp. He told him to pick it up and walk.[31]

When Jesus heals the emotional wounds of the past, He does the whole job; something we are unable to do for ourselves.

---

[31] Mark 2:1-12

After Jesus makes us whole, our addictions and compulsive behaviors disappear, never to return. We have personally experienced His healing and witnessed it more times than we can count.

When we talk about healing, we are not talking about the cure of a so-called "disease of addiction," but about the healing of addiction's underlying spiritual and emotional causes, especially our sense of powerlessness.

When we clean the inside of the cup, the outside becomes clean as well.

When the root of addiction is gone, addictive behavior ceases.

Addiction is not permanent. We can become free.

We need help to do it. No one recovers alone.

You are not alone.

How Do We Become Whole?

How do we become whole? How do we help others become whole?

Wholeness and freedom come through:

- ❖ Spiritual rebirth
- ❖ Cognitive Regeneration
- ❖ The healing restoration of our souls
- ❖ The development of mature spiritual fruit

Spiritual Rebirth: There is a legion of competing doctrines within Christianity. Rather than present a detailed theological exposition, we will simply bullet point what we mean by spiritual rebirth.

Spiritual rebirth simply means we are born a second time when we accept Jesus' offer of friendship.

What it means to become Jesus' friend:

- ❖ We have repented of our sin, asked for, and received Jesus' forgiveness.

- ❖ Our soul becomes alive as Jesus takes up residence in our hearts.

- ❖ We become a permanent citizen of God's kingdom and a member of God's family.

- ❖ We rely on the Holy Spirit for comfort, counsel, and the power to live the life we were born to live.

- ❖ We come to know our Father in Heaven as He is; loving, not wrathful.

- ❖ As we walk in genuine, Christ-centered love, our hearts turn outward. We begin to care about others at least as much as we care about ourselves.

- ❖ Love motivates us to do what we can to relieve the pain and suffering of others.

- ❖ As we grow in our friendship with Jesus, we become more like Him, exhibiting the fruit of the Holy Spirit: love, joy, peace, patience, kindness, goodness, faithfulness, gentleness, and self-control.

- ❖ We become peacemakers.

Cognitive Regeneration: To regenerate means to rejuvenate, revive, renew, or bring back to life.

Cognitive Regeneration is a Christ-centered, Holy Spirit-led process of discovery and personal empowerment.

It encourages inner transformation through the renewing of our minds. It engages the intellect, the heart, and the spirit.

Cognitive Regeneration transforms us from the inside out.

Romans 12:2 "And do not be conformed to this world, but be transformed by the renewing of your mind, so that you may prove what the will of God is, that which is good and acceptable and complete."

Ideally, someone with empathy, who enjoys a deep and meaningful relationship with Jesus, is led by the Holy Spirit and is willing to share their joys and sufferings with those they try to help will facilitate the regeneration process.

Over time a relationship of love and trust is established, and healing comes.

Cognitive Therapy: We mention Cognitive Therapy only to contrast it with Cognitive Regeneration. While there are some similarities between them, they are fundamentally different.

Cognitive Therapy is <u>not</u> Christ-centered. It is a secular approach that atheists, agnostics, and people of other faiths are most likely to pursue.[32]

To cognate means: to think, reason, or remember.

------

[32] The *My Recovery Community* does not offer Cognitive Therapy. We offer Cognitive Regeneration.

Cognitive Therapy is a process of self-discovery and self-diagnosis, facilitated by a mental health professional rather than a minister of the gospel. It engages the intellect, and at least to some degree, the heart.

It has value, though it will not bring complete healing. Cognitive Therapy can help people function and cope with their pain and circumstances.

The Healing Restoration of the Soul: Seeking restoration and healing from Jesus is unlikely to be a path atheists, agnostics, and people of other faiths will take unless desperation and the failure of alternatives bring them to it.

We understand desperation. And failure. Been there, done that.

Traumatic events, especially those occurring in childhood, can damage our mental and emotional health and cause us pain.

Most, if not all of us, suffer trauma at least once in our lives and live with the pain trauma produces.

Traumas may be as unexpected as the sudden death of a loved one, a disabling accident, a parent's incarceration, or a divorce.

Other traumas occur over time, such as consistently being told we are stupid or worthless, always being the last to be chosen to join a team, food scarcity, rejection, abandonment, or childhood neglect.

Traumas can cause us to believe lies about God, ourselves, other people, and how life is supposed to work.

The memory of a trauma we've suffered becomes the container for a lie we believe. It is the lie that resonates in our souls. It is the lie that continues to cause us pain.

"I'm stupid." "I'm alone." "No one will take care of me." "Even God doesn't love me."

These are examples of the types of lies we may believe.

The Church is supposed to be a hospital for wounded souls, where people can come for healing. We often fail to fulfill this role.

Our answers for pervasive emotional pain have frequently been ineffective and even damaging.

Dispensing judgment and legalism, rather than offering grace and mercy, can create even more trauma, plant more lies, and leave people feeling more wounded and abandoned than before.

May we repent of such things and change our ways.

Good news - the healing of our souls is possible through what we call "revelation truth," when God speaks to us in our hearts.

Revelation truth is the "aha" moment when something suddenly becomes clear, or more apparent to us than it was before.

It's as if we've always known it!

John 8:32 "You will know the truth, and the truth will make you free."

People may tell us the truth, but that doesn't mean we will believe them. Human beings are often wrong. We may reject what someone tells us and miss our healing.

But when we receive revelation truth from God, we believe it, and we are changed.

How do we receive revelation truth?

If we are willing to hear from God, we will receive it in whatever way He chooses to speak to us.

When God speaks, we believe what He says. Even people who, until that moment, didn't believe in Him, believe Him.

We receive the truth, and He who is the truth sets us free.

> Dawn: I have received revelation truth and healing through worship, music, reading good books, prayer, the counsel of others, and by being quiet in the presence of the Lord.
>
> How do I know it was Jesus who spoke to me in my heart?
>
> I was changed. Healing, freedom, and the restoration of my soul was the fruit of that change.

That God speaks to people today may ruffle a few feathers.

That God might heal people of a lifetime of emotional trauma in a matter of minutes, with a few words, is outside the realm of possibility to many people.

We have personally experienced it, and have witnessed the miraculous healing of others, more times than we can count.

If anyone wants to argue concerning whether the healing we've described is real and really from God, or nitpick over doctrines, methods, and processes, feel free. We will abstain.

While others bicker, we will keep serving people in pain, and continue to enjoy the healing we've personally received.

No doubt, others whom God has healed will be doing the same.

When Jesus heals, it's a done deal. The emotional wounds that set us up for destruction are erased in moments, never to return.

Things that years of secular therapies could not make a dent in, including issues "solved" by mood-altering prescription pain medication, are rooted out, once and for all.

Addictive behavior is a manifestation of a heart problem.

Human beings do not understand what is in our hearts.

If we did, we could solve all the world's problems. Everyone would be happy, whole, and free.

Poverty, war, violence, selfishness, greed - all these evils and more, would disappear from our planet for good.

But they haven't.

We do not know what is in our hearts. How then can we possibly fix whatever is in there?

We can't, but God can - if we let Him.

God knows our pain and how to heal it. For some, healing may come through Cognitive Regeneration. For others, He may speak a healing revelation truth. Or He may do both.

He may also use other means to bring healing. Whatever He does, He does in a manner of His choosing.

Whatever His methods, the outcome is the same. We are made whole. It is too marvelous for words.

Once an addict, always an addict? Not so. Permanent healing is not only possible; it is God's desire!

The Development of Mature Spiritual Fruit: One of the most common frustrations shared by those who come to us for help, is that other people always tell them what to do.

Dawn: When someone expresses this frustration, I often ask:

"Would you like it if no one ever had a problem with you again? Would you like it if no one ever told you what to do ever again?"

The answer is always;

"Yes! That is what I want!"

Imagine. No more going to court. Family members stop monitoring your every move. Your parents stop telling you what to do.

It becomes possible as we grow spiritually fruitful and mature.

Galatians 5:22-23 "But the fruit of the Spirit is love, joy, peace, patience, kindness, goodness, faithfulness, gentleness, self-control; against such things, there is no law."

Imagine: if you were loving, joyful, peaceful, patient, kind, good, faithful, gentle, and had self-control, would anyone have a problem with you?

If your character, attitudes, and behavior were evidence of the Holy Spirit's presence and influence in your life, would anyone be afraid you might hurt or disappoint them?

Would you abuse yourself or anyone else? Would anyone have a problem with you, or feel compelled to tell you what to do?

Of course not, unless they were control freaks in need of their healing.

If you read the Apostle Paul's letter to the Galatians in the Bible, you will see the fruit of the Spirit only manifests in us if we are friends with Jesus.

We receive the Holy Spirit from Jesus. We come to know our Father in Heaven through Jesus.

Jesus gives us new life, renews our minds, and restores our souls.

John 15:4-5 "Abide in Me, and I in you. As the branch cannot bear fruit of itself unless it abides in the vine, so neither can you, unless you abide in Me.

"I am the vine, you are the branches; he who abides in Me and I in him, he bears much fruit, for apart from Me, you can do nothing."

The evidence of God's work and presence in us is that we produce good fruit.

If we are bearing good fruit, then no one should have a problem with us. We can take comfort in the knowledge. It is likely their issue, not ours, if they still have a problem with us.

The fruit of the Spirit remains no matter what our situation may be. The real fruit withstands stress and difficulties, while self-manufactured fruit, maintained by our effort, evaporates and is exposed as a counterfeit.

The first fruit is love. We could probably say the only fruit of the Spirit is love. The fruit listed after love are all expressions or attributes of love.

The goal of all recovery programs is for addicts to gain self-control; to stop using. The goal for the family is similar; to cease trying to impose self-discipline on uncooperative addicts.

Self-control is the outcome of possessing the eight fruit that precede it. Leapfrogging over the first fruit to achieve self-control doesn't work all that well.

The fruit of the Spirit is progressive. The development of each fruit depends on the activation of the previous fruit.

- ❖ We cannot be joyful until we know we are loved.

- ❖ We cannot be peaceful until we are joyful.

- ❖ We cannot be patient until we are peaceful.

- ❖ We cannot be kind until we are patient.

- ❖ We cannot be good until we are kind.

- ❖ We cannot be faithful until we are good.

- ❖ We cannot be gentle until we are faithful.

- ❖ We cannot exercise self-control until we are gentle.

The strength to resist temptation comes from the Spirit of God, and rests on the healing Jesus has brought into our lives.

Galatians 5:16 "But I say, walk by the Spirit, and you will not carry out the desires of the flesh."

In freedom, we retain our right to make our own choices.

We freely chose to rely on God no matter what circumstances we may be in.

Galatians 5:18 "But if you are led by the Spirit, you are not under the Law."

We no longer self-medicate or blame people, places, or things for our condition. Instead, we seek the One who cares for our souls for strength, comfort, and healing.

Freedom is about love, expressed through relationships with God and others.

As we have said before, building loving, healthy relationships takes time.

Ultimately, becoming whole is about growing up to become an emotionally healthy, spiritually mature human being.

Then you will experience true freedom in Christ.

And no one will need to tell you what to do!

True freedom is the capacity to live
and enjoy life no matter what
comes. It means we are powerful,
but we temper our power with love.

PRINCIPLE SIX:
TRUE FREEDOM
BEGINS WITH CHRIST

True, lasting freedom begins when we accept Jesus' offer of friendship.

As the fruit of genuine love becomes more evident in us, we leave immaturity behind, become the person we were born to be, and live the life we were born to live.

We uncover the gifts God has given us and use them for the benefit of others.

True Freedom

True freedom does not mean we will always get everything right. Nor does it mean we will never suffer pain or loss ever again. We will make mistakes. We will be hurt and will sometimes hurt others.

True freedom is the capacity to live and enjoy life no matter what comes. It means we are powerful, but we temper our power with love.

Selfishness in Recovery

Conventional wisdom says addicts must be selfish about their recovery. While recovery ought to be our top priority, telling people to be selfish about it takes it too far.

Addicts don't need to be encouraged to be selfish. They are already selfish, to the point of causing harm to others.

Addicts frequently lack an essential character trait called empathy. They are often too self-centered to notice or care about other's pain, including the pain they cause.

Addicts care most about one thing; getting their next fix.

Empathy is a sign of genuine recovery. If we have stopped using but are not empathetic, we are only on a "dry drunk." We are still active addicts on the inside.

Hebrews 13:3 "Remember the prisoners, as if in prison with them."

Empathy is the ability to put ourselves in the shoes of others and feel their joys and sorrows. When others celebrate, we rejoice with them. When others suffer loss, we suffer along with them

It is as if these things were happening to us, except that it is not about us. It is about them.

Without empathy, we become more selfish as our addictions take hold and take over. We become the center of a tiny world; the only thing in it that matters.

It is possible to remain selfish and successfully stop using, but our sobriety is unlikely to last for very long. We will struggle with our recovery, and never see freedom, until we gain the ability to empathize.

Sympathy Versus Empathy

When we hear someone has "gone back out there," we tend to respond in one of three ways. One is sympathy; another is empathy, but the most frequent response is judgment.

Sympathy and empathy are not the same. The story about the good Samaritan perfectly illustrates the difference:

Luke 10:30-37 Jesus replied and said, "A man was going down from Jerusalem to Jericho and fell among robbers. They stripped him, and beat him, and went away, leaving him half dead.

"By chance, a priest was going down on that road, and when he saw him, he passed by on the other side. Likewise, a Levite also, when he came to the place and saw him, passed by on the other side.

"But a Samaritan who was on a journey came upon him; and when he saw him, he felt compassion, and came to him and bandaged up his wounds, pouring oil and wine on them; and he put him on his beast, and brought him to an inn and took care of him.

"On the next day, he took out two denarii, gave them to the innkeeper, and said, 'Take care of him; and whatever more you spend, when I return I will repay you.'

"Which of these three do you think proved to be a neighbor to the man who fell into the robbers' hands?"

And he said, "The one who showed mercy toward him." Then Jesus said to him, "Go and do the same."

Sympathy feels sorry for people in distress but does nothing to help them, beyond a pat on the back and a few token words of rote comfort.

Sympathy thinks, but does not say out loud, "better them than me."

Sympathy risks nothing and costs nothing. Sympathy is selfish.

It is about how <u>we</u> feel about someone else's misfortune.

Empathy is not about how we feel, but about how someone else feels. It can be risky and costly. It compels us to do what we can to relieve the suffering of others.

Empathetic people do not think of themselves as heroes, nor do they boast about their good works. They perform their deeds of service quietly, in the shade, expecting nothing in return.

Empathy is a manifestation of love. Love is not selfish.

Many of us were incapable of empathy or genuine love in the early days of our recovery. We were selfish before addiction took over.

Addiction made us even more self-centered and childish.

We wanted what we wanted when we wanted it.

If we choose to let go of our selfishness, we will become empathetic as we become whole.

Sympathy, which is nothing more than making socially-acceptable noises without active engagement, will make way for genuine caring.

We will become less selfish and our universe will expand.

Small Universe = Big Problems

Rather than explore and enjoy the incredible, almost limitless variety of human experiences, addicts focus on just one thing; getting the next fix.

Our laser-like focus on using doesn't allow for experiences that broaden our horizons and make our lives meaningful and exciting.

We settle for a meaningless, powerless life, instead of enjoying the meaningful, powerful life we were born to live.

Addiction and its attendant selfishness make our universe very small. Everything in it revolves around us. Other peoples' problems do not concern us, but our own certainly do.

Living in a small, self-centered world makes our problems seem much worse than they are. But when examined in the context of a vast universe of endless possibilities, our issues seem smaller and manageable.

We can look at them and say, "This isn't so bad. I'm not the only one who has had to deal with this."

Instead, our pothole-sized difficulties become Grand Canyons of pain. We lose hope, become depressed, and give up trying to resolve our issues.

It doesn't occur to us to ask for help unless it's the kind that enables us to keep using.

Living in a small and selfish universe strengthens our sense of powerlessness and pushes us deeper into the pit of addiction.

Living in a vast universe, where we are not the only one who matters, makes our problems right-sized and manageable.

We are less likely to be overwhelmed by them. We face problems and move on.

A small world is a prison where we die. A vast world is a place to live in freedom.

That is our choice; to die in slavery or live in freedom.

Full freedom is possible. What's your pleasure?

Temporary versus Permanent Pleasure

Human beings are seekers of pleasure.

We seek it because we do not already possess it. If we possessed <u>real</u> pleasure, we would not need to seek it!

Many of us became addicts in our pursuit of pleasure.

We found trouble instead of fun. We found addiction instead of freedom.

2nd Peter 2:19 "For by what a man is overcome, by this he is enslaved. "

We want to feel good all the time. If we were rock-bottom honest, most of us would admit many of our prayers are some version of this:

"Dear Lord...give me a safe, easy, and comfortable life, from birth to death...amen."

We seek <u>permanent</u> pleasure, but all this world can offer us is <u>temporary</u> pleasure.

Hebrews 11:24-25 "By faith Moses, when he had grown up, refused to be called the son of Pharaoh's daughter, choosing to endure ill-treatment with the people of God than to enjoy the <u>passing pleasures</u> of sin."

The adopted son of the ruler of Egypt, Moses was a member of the wealthiest, most powerful family on earth. He had access to all the pleasures money and power could buy. He might even have become the next ruler of Egypt!

But Moses rejected temporary pleasure, led the Hebrew people out of slavery, and wandered in the wilderness for forty years.

Psalm 16:11 "You will make known to me the path of life; in Your presence is fullness of joy. Your right-hand holds <u>pleasures forever</u>."

Though he did not enter the Promised Land himself, Moses ultimately enjoyed the permanent pleasure found in Christ.

The pleasure we enjoy through our friendship with Jesus is permanent; it continues throughout this life and into the next.

We pay a high price for temporary pleasure:

Proverbs 14:12 "There is a way that seems right to a man, but in the end, it leads to death."

Christ paid the highest price - His life - so we can enjoy permanent pleasure:

John 3:16 "For God so loved the world that He gave His only Son, that whoever believes in Him shall not die, but have eternal life."

Addiction is a temporary pleasure that soon loses its "feel good." It robs us of our freedom and denies us the permanent pleasure we might otherwise enjoy.

Temporary pleasure is a counterfeit pleasure.

Permanent pleasure is the real thing.

Freedom brings us permanent pleasure.

As we have said before, recovery is good. It is just not complete.

Freedom is complete.

Whether you're an addict or someone who loves one, you have the same decision to make; do I settle for recovery, or do I press on to freedom?

No one can make this decision for you, nor should anyone try to force you to decide in favor of one or the other.

The choice is entirely yours.

How to Accept Jesus' Offer of Friendship

Revelation 3:20 "Behold, I stand at the door and knock; if anyone hears My voice and opens the door, I will come in to him and will dine with him, and he with Me."

We are sure many of our readers have already accepted Jesus' offer of friendship and are on their way through recovery to freedom in Christ.

We're also sure many people have wandered away from God and have been living in the wilderness. You may be wondering whether there is any way to come home. You may believe there isn't.

We are happy to tell you that's a lie. No matter what you may have done, God wants to welcome you home.

You may have walked away from Jesus, but He did not walk away from you. He waits with open arms to embrace you.

Romans 8:38-39 "For I am persuaded that neither death, nor life, nor angels, nor principalities, nor things present, nor things to come, nor powers, nor height, nor depth, nor any other created thing, will be able to separate us from God's love, which is in Christ Jesus our Lord."

If you have not yet accepted His offer of friendship and are interested in knowing how to do it, it is very simple:

Romans 10:9-11 "If you confess with your mouth Jesus as Lord and believe in your heart that God raised Him from the dead, you will be saved; for with the heart a person believes, resulting in freedom from guilt and sin, and with the mouth, he confesses, resulting in deliverance from the power of sin.

"For the Scripture says, "Whoever believes in Him will not be disappointed."

Jesus did all the heavy lifting when He surrendered His life on the cross and then walked out of the grave alive three days later. He did it because He loves us, even though we didn't always love or believe in Him.

Would you like to be free from guilt and sin? Would you like to be delivered from the power of sin?

Many people begin or renew their life in Christ with a simple prayer. There are no rules concerning the "right words" to say.

The Holy Spirit will help you; just say whatever is in your heart.

You might pray something like this:

Dear Lord Jesus,

I have sinned. I am tired of living only for myself. I want to love the way. You love and become the person I was born to be.

I ask You to forgive me for everything I have done, said, or believed that caused You and others pain. Help me also to forgive those who have harmed me.

Help me to hear Your voice when You speak to me in my heart.

Help me walk with you in love and friendship all my days. Come live in my heart and show me how to live in You.

I love You, Lord; thank You for loving me first and best, even when I didn't love or believe in You.

I pray this in Jesus' name. Amen.

A New Life of Freedom

When our heart believes, and our mouth confesses our belief, we announce to all we are starting over on a new foundation.

That doesn't mean we're going to do everything right from now on. We will still make mistakes along the way. But there is a difference; we are no longer alone!

There is now someone living in us who loves us and knows us better than we know ourselves; someone who will lead, encourage, and challenge us; the Holy Spirit, who gives us comfort, counsel, and the power to live our new life.[33]

We will also come to know our Father in Heaven as He is. He's just like Jesus. As Jesus said:

John 14:9 "He who has seen Me has seen the Father."

Conversation with God – Hearing His Voice

Being Jesus' friend means we can have a conversation with Him any time, not just when we're in church.

He hears us perfectly, but it takes time for us to recognize His voice and know when He is speaking to us.

Hearing God's voice is not supposed to be a rare experience reserved only for a small number of especially "holy people."

It is supposed to be part of an everyday relationship with God.

---

[33] Christians don't always agree about how and when we receive the Holy Spirit. We think all Christians can agree that living a Christ-centered life is not possible without empowerment by the Holy Spirit.

He speaks, we listen; we speak, He listens - like a conversation with any good friend.

It may take time to learn how to hear God's voice. That's okay.

God wants us to hear Him and understand what He says.[34]

Transformed from the Inside Out

Before we knew Jesus, we looked like this:

2nd Timothy 3:2-4 "For people will be lovers of self, lovers of money, boastful, arrogant, revilers, disobedient to parents, ungrateful, unholy, unloving, irreconcilable, malicious gossips, without self-control, brutal, haters of good, treacherous, reckless, conceited, lovers of pleasure rather than lovers of God."

But after we accept Jesus' offer of friendship, we begin to look like Him:

Galatians 5:22-23 "But the fruit of the Spirit is love, joy, peace, patience, kindness, goodness, faithfulness, gentleness, self-control; against such things, there is no law."

God offers us an abundant, full, meaningful life; He does not force it on us. We are not talking about wealth, fame, or the other temporary pleasures of life, but about living each moment of our lives as fully as possible.

This offer is free. You only have to decide whether to accept it.

---

[34] We recommend an excellent book by Les Carroll: *The Languages of God*. It is available from Amazon.

OLD WINE TO NEW WINE:
RICHARD'S JOURNEY TO WHOLENESS

**"I used to drink the old wine - no, I wasn't very smart.
Today I drink the new wine and have Jesus in my heart."**[35]

There are approximately 24 million addicts in the United States.

Only one addict in ten seeks help for their addiction. Of these, only one achieves permanent sobriety. In other words, out of one hundred addicts, only one enjoys lifelong sobriety.

I am that one. Here is my story.

Early Struggles

When I was very young, our family lived in public housing until my mother managed to move us into a lovely apartment near Harvard Square in Cambridge, Massachusetts.

Money was tight in those early years. When we couldn't afford to buy heating oil, we ran the gas oven with the door open.

---

[35] *Old Wine, New Wine*; a song by Richard "Stonefingers" Johnson available at kerithresources.com.

Candles got us through the evenings when the electricity was off. When we ran out of food, the welfare lady brought some.

The government peanut butter was good, but I still couldn't tell you what was in those cans of pink mystery meat! It tasted terrible, no matter how we cooked it. The only way to eat it was to fry it, drown it in ketchup, and hope for the best.

1957: A Very Bad Year

Losing My Father: First, my father left. I do not know whether he abandoned us, or my mother kicked him out. I only knew he was gone.

Over the next ten years, I rarely saw him. I grew to hate him.

Sexual Assault: That same year, a relative kidnapped me, took me to New York City for a few days, molested me, and then brought me home and dumped me on my mother's doorstep.

I was five years old, too young to grasp what had happened to me. I just knew it was terrible.

I buried the memory of it, but the pain and anger kept popping up over the decades that followed.

Whenever a memory pushed to surface, I buried it again.

These two traumas opened the door for the spirit of powerless to establish a foothold in my life. They also turned me inward.

Introvert

I was a quiet child who loved to read, play the piano, go to church on Sunday, and attend school.

Scholastically, I was ahead of my peers in the first grade (and bored), so they sent me back to the kindergarten class to read to the younger kids.

I spent hours after school in the library. Some nights, staffers had to search the stacks to tell me the place was closing, and it was time to go home.

I got a scholarship to study at the New England Conservatory of Music in Boston. I loved spending Saturdays there, playing the piano, and learning music theory.

If I couldn't be a history professor at Harvard University, I decided I wanted to be a composer and orchestra conductor.

Then the Beatles came along. Their influence and the "folk music scare" of the early sixties led me to abandon my classical music dreams. I quit the conservatory and picked up the guitar.

Being bullied in junior high drove me deeper into myself. I was a lover, not a fighter, though I won the only fight I couldn't avoid.

After that, the other kids left me alone.

High school was boring. At the start of my sophomore year, there were only two kids who smoked dope in our urban school, and we knew each other.

Before school ended for the summer, there were hundreds of kids getting high with us.

243

The Summer of Love

I discovered the pleasures of alcohol, drugs, and free love in 1967. I was fifteen.

My first drink was a can of Colt 45 malt liquor stolen from a neighbor's refrigerator.

My first drug was a joint my younger brother shared with me one cold October night on the ferry to Martha's Vineyard Island.

I lost my virginity to a girl I'd known since the first grade. It happened under a bush on the banks of the Charles River.

It was the Summer of Love. The hippie thing was going strong, making its way from San Francisco to Harvard Square.

I lived on the streets, going home only when I ran out of money, food, or needed a bath.

I was there during the Harvard Square riots when police tear-gassed and chased protesters through my neighborhood.

I briefly sold LSD and grass, until some tough characters informed me I was out of business. I agreed with them.

A kid I knew from school did not. The police found his body in the trash.

I've known a lot of people who died for substance abuse-related reasons. He was the first. Today I tell the men I mentor I know a lot of dead people. In many of the circles I used to run in, I am the last man standing.

Most of my friends went to Woodstock. I didn't. I'm still glad I didn't go. I'm not a big fan of mud - or crowds

Killing a Perfectly Good Music Career

The Boston folk music scene was going strong in the sixties.

From the very first weekend it opened, I hung out at the Nameless Coffeehouse in Harvard Square, where I became a regular performer.

I was there the night Jay Leno performed. The folk music purists in the audience booed him. They only liked people with guitars.

My manager owned Passim Coffeehouse in Cambridge. He did a lot for me, but I didn't appreciate it at the time. Bob Donlin was an excellent judge of talent. He taught me a lot about performing.

Thanks to my growing substance abuse, Bob grew tired of dealing with my nonsense and tore up our contract. Rather than sue him, I paid him off. Then I bad-mouthed him to everyone.

No one else wanted to manage my career, including people who encouraged me to break my contract with Bob and go with them.

It was years before I figured out why. They all heard the ugly things I was saying about Bob. No one wanted to be the target of that kind of rage.

A few years after I got clean and sober, I had an opportunity to sit down with Bob, tell him what I had been saying about him, and ask for his forgiveness.

He was far more gracious and forgiving than I deserved.

Bob died a few years later. He was a caring and generous man.

Without a manager, I was no longer an opening act on the college concert circuit, hanging out and getting high with well-known musicians and comedians.

The only work I could get was singing in bars for fifty bucks a night and all I could drink. I often slept in my car behind the gin mills where I played.

I took sponge baths in the men's room in the morning and then roamed around town until the sun went down.

I grew increasingly angry and resentful.

God's Sense of Humor: There was a bar in New Hampshire, where I played every few months. They paid me well because I packed the place. A biker I'll call Joe allowed me to sleep on his sofa whenever I was in town.

Early one Sunday morning, a couple of guys knocked on the door. Joe let them in. They were evangelists from a local church.

One of them cornered Joe in the kitchen while the other one talked to my back as I laid on the couch, feigning sleep. He sat on the coffee table right on top of my dope bag. If he noticed the loaded handgun sitting there next to him, he didn't say so.

He wouldn't shut up, not even when I pretended to snore.

After they finally left, Joe and I stood around in the kitchen and cracked a couple of beers open. We told each other we agreed with everything those two guys said. We just didn't like the way they barged in and beat us up with it.

Years later, I was ministering on a Sunday morning at a church in that same town.

When I told the congregation the last time I was in their town, a couple of guys came to Joe's house and shared the gospel with us, two men in the back row started shouting "Hallelujah."

It was those same two guys!

No one can tell me God doesn't have a sense of humor.

A Universe of Lies

As my life spiraled downward, selfishness made my universe very small. I became incapable of empathy and genuine love. I got good at faking friendship.

If I called someone a friend, it was only because they were useful to me. When they were no longer useful, I got rid of them and found someone else to take their place.

I had different sets of lies for different sets of people. I worked hard to prevent people from one group from meeting people from another. I was afraid my con game would be exposed if they compared notes.

When my drug and alcohol abuse became bad enough, I lost track. My system began to break down. I started telling the wrong lies to the wrong people and got funny looks in response.

Drinking, drugs, and narcissism destroyed a promising career in the music business. I was given many opportunities to make a success of it and blew them all.

That turned out to be a blessing.

I thought of myself as a nice guy who never hurt anybody. The reality was different. I hurt a lot of people; more people than I can remember. My nice guy self-image was another lie.

I was in terrible emotional pain, but I couldn't admit it. I kept drinking and drugging to keep myself mellow.

People sometimes told me I was the angriest man they knew. I bit their heads off, denying it.

The End is Near

I started to feel as if life wasn't worth living and tried to kill myself a couple of times "by accident."

After finishing up a week performing at that New Hampshire bar I mentioned earlier, partying until three or four in the morning, I jumped in my pickup truck and headed for home, driving south along the shore of a nearby lake.

There was a sharp curve in the road where the speed limit dropped to twenty-five miles per hour.

They meant it. Just beyond the curve was a cliff. If you went too fast, you could drive off the cliff and land in the lake.

More than once, I turned off the headlights and hit the gas when I came to that curve. I got through it every time on screeching tires.

That I'm still here to write about it is a miracle. I sometimes wonder whether a couple of big, beefy angels pushed hard to keep my truck on the road.

Recovery, Pain, and an Encounter with Jesus

Turning Wine into Water: On December 31st, 1979, I went out to get drunk on New Years' Eve with my girlfriend. It didn't matter how much I drank that night; I couldn't get a buzz.

My drinking pattern encouraged variety. I used to drink gin and tonic for a week, then peppermint schnapps for a week, then stout, porter, or beer for a week, then whiskey for a week.

That night I mixed and drank them all, one right after the other.

I couldn't get a buzz. I went home before midnight, stone-cold sober. That was the last time I drank or did drugs.

A few weeks later, I was walking past a church just before noon. A side door was open. I went in.

There was an AA meeting getting ready to start. Before I could turn around to leave, a couple of guys called my name. They sat me down at the table and put a cup of coffee in my hand.

The meeting started. Someone rapped a gavel on the table and said; "My name is _____, and I'm an alcoholic." The next guy gave his name and said the same thing. And the next.

It was coming around to me. I didn't know what to do. I wanted to leave, but it wouldn't have been polite. I'd drunk their coffee.

When my turn came, I said, "My name is Richard, and I'm an alcoholic." I put my head down on the table and started to cry.

They were tears of relief, not pain. For the first time, I said out loud what my heart already knew.

I spent the next two years attending as many AA meetings as I could, sometimes as many as three a day. I got a sponsor, read the Big Book, worked the twelve steps, and did everything else they told me to do.

I was happy for the first time in years. I began to feel alive again. I put the guitars away and got a steady job.

Hitting the Wall: AA mentions a moment when no power on earth will keep us from picking up a drink.

I hit that moment - hard.

The woman I had lived with for several years decided I wasn't fun anymore. She traded me in for a younger model.

The shock of a sudden end to our relationship triggered intense emotional pain. I was not at all ready to deal with it.

I moved out of her house. I kept going to meetings and somehow managed to stay employed. I was crazy with grief and anger.

I called my ex several times, told her I loved her, then threatened to kill her. I didn't understand why she hung up!

Other times I jumped in my car, scattered gravel as I roared into her driveway at three in the morning, banged on her door, and threatened to kill her if she didn't let me in.

I didn't understand why she wouldn't let me in.

It's a miracle she didn't call the cops. Years later, I came to realize our relationship was toxic. Had it continued, I might have missed fulfilling my destiny.

I was still furious at the Lord. I blamed Him for everything that had gone wrong in my life. I told people God did not exist. It was a feeble attempt to get even with Him.

An Encounter with Jesus: The pain became unbearable. On the afternoon of January 24th, 1982, I shut myself in my bedroom closet, grabbed the clothes rod, and tried to break it.

It wouldn't break. In the dark, I cried out, "God, I can't live this way another second."

Jesus showed up.

I didn't see a glowing figure wearing a white robe with a halo over His head, nor was there a voice I could hear with my ears.

The presence of the Living God filled the closet. I heard Him speak in my heart. I don't remember what He said or how long I was in that closet, but when I came out, things had changed.

The pain was gone, replaced by an indescribable peace. It was like pulling the stopper on a bathtub full of dirty water and watching it flow away down the drain. In a matter of minutes, Jesus healed me (though there was much more healing to come). Opinions I had held for years changed.

I knew my life was no longer my own, and that was fine. Jesus bought and paid for me. My new ambition was to make sure He got His money's worth.

Beyond Recovery to Freedom in Christ

Galatians 5:1 "It was for freedom that Christ set us free; therefore, stand firm, and do not be subject again to a yoke of slavery."

Not long after my "moment of decision" passed, Jesus kicked me out of Alcoholics Anonymous. I haven't been back since. AA helped me stop using, but they did not make me whole. Jesus did that.

Nonetheless, I am grateful for the start AA gave me.

251

A Restored Relationship with My Dad: I started to visit my father, where he worked. We had many good conversations.

He told me where he had been all the years he was missing.

I grew to love him and was able to forgive him. Forgiveness set me free. Jesus made that possible.

Dad lived with me just before I got married. He hadn't changed in many ways. He still liked to drink and blow all his money on the race track. It didn't bother me.

Dad moved out on my wedding day. We put on our tuxedos and drove to the church. He packed his few possessions in his gym bag and took it with him.

After the wedding ceremony, he caught a ride to Boston with my brother, and my wife moved in.

Dad and I became close while we lived together, and closer still in the years that followed.

Before he died, he surrendered his life to the Lord. His last words to me were, "It's a new family now."

I still wear the watch he gave me.

The Lord eventually told me to take the guitars out of the closet. I began to write again, but now the songs were about Him.

I used to write tunes with titles like; "If You Talk in Your Sleep, Don't Cheat on Your Old Lady."

Now I write about the incredible love and mercy of God.

I Married My Best Friend's Daughter: I married the love of my life, Dawn Marie, in 1985. I was nervous the first time I kissed her. I didn't know how her father would react.

When he found out we were an item, he told Dawn it was about time she brought home a man he liked!

While our marriage has endured testing over the years, the Lord has sustained and strengthened us. I am more in love with her than on the day we said, "We do, no matter what."

More Forgiveness and Healing: Years after becoming sober, clean, and getting reacquainted with Jesus, the Lord began to peel the onion of pain associated with the sexual assault I suffered at the age of five.

With Jesus' help, I began to remember the details of the assault. The emotions I had suppressed, especially the anger, came surging to the surface.

This time I didn't run away. When I faced my pain, I discovered I was 75% of the way to my healing!

With my wife's love and support, I walked through the rest of the anger until I got to the forgiveness. Forgiveness broke the back of the evil done to me. I was free!

The conventional wisdom says victims of sexual abuse and assault are stuck with the pain of it for life. Healing is not possible, they say; we will never get over it.

Like "once an addict, always an addict," this too is a lie. We can be made whole. I know what forgiveness is, but that's a story for another time.

I can sincerely say I have forgiven the man who hurt me. Today

I am free of the anger and pain I stuffed inside for years. I have my power back.

Called to Minister to Society's Outcasts

For almost ten years beginning in the nineties, Dawn Marie and I, our kids, Suzanna and Jimmy, our dog, Jasper, and a succession of pet hamsters, lived in a fifth-wheel trailer in church parking lots all over North America.

We ministered in prisons, jails, juvenile detention centers, residential re-entry facilities, churches, and many other venues.

We met a lot of people, made a lot of friends, and saw a lot of things that worked to help people get free and stay free.

I was ordained in 1995 and commissioned as a Bishop and Apostle in 2017. Pretty amazing for an old, burned-out hippie!

We came off the road in 2005, bought a home in southern Indiana near Louisville, Kentucky, and started Christian Formation Ministries.

Our purpose was to bring life, hope, and healing to inmates, addicts, their children, and immediate family members, as well as other people in pain.

Jesus has been very good to us. Love surrounds us - our volunteers, Community Chaplains, and the kids and adults who have become part of our extended family.

The kids call me Papa Bear.

Change is a Constant: In 2018, our ministry completed a three-year leadership transition to the next generation.

Reverend. Suzanna Jacobson, our daughter, now sits in the big chair, bringing fresh energy, enthusiasm, and vision to the work. Dawn and I are still very much involved, happy we are no longer running things.

What More Does Anyone Need?

1ˢᵗ Corinthians 2:9 "Things which eye has not seen, and ear has not heard, and which have not entered the heart of man; all that, God has prepared for those who love Him."

I can truthfully say I am having the time of my life.

I am married to a wonderful woman, have two remarkable adult children, and three grandkids (so far) who give us a great deal of joy and keep us on our toes.

Flawed as I am, I get to hang out with the Lord. Every morning, I ask Him:

"What are you doing today, Jesus? Can I do it with you?"

He always says yes.

Jesus has given me much more than I could have imagined or asked.

May He do the same for you.

Jesus can break every chain.

RAISED TO BE AN ENABLER: DAWN'S JOURNEY TO WHOLENESS

When people ask about my childhood, I tell them I had a happy one. I grew up believing I was special.

I was the apple of my father's eye. I knew I was loved.

But if you ask me to share things that adversely impacted my emotional well-being, my childhood becomes a bit less than ideal.

Before I received healing from the Lord, I was always able to justify my bad choices and painful behaviors to myself and others. Since my healing, I no longer need to defend those things.

The things we focus on when we tell our stories matters. What we think, feel, and believe about events of the past affects how we respond to things that happen to us today.

I hope you will identify with my story.

The steps I have taken, and the process I have gone through to secure healing for myself and my family, may help you gain insight into your struggles, past and present, as you begin your journey to wholeness.

These are Not the Parents We are Looking For

A close friend once told me:

"When you think about your childhood, remember, the parents you grew up with, and the parents you have today, are not the same people."

She was right.

Lessons from My Mother: My mother, and adept enabler, raised me to be an enabler, too. She learned how to be one during her childhood, just as I did.

My grandparents, two of my favorite people, were wonderful to me. They were also alcoholics.

Growing up in a home with two alcoholic parents made my mother chronically fearful, with a desperate need for approval, and a deep well of suppressed anger. She carried her pain into adulthood.

As a child, I was terrified of upsetting my mother. Her moods were unpredictable, sometimes so intense, they seemed to fill the whole house.

I developed an ability to quickly and accurately assess what kind of day my mother was having, even if I couldn't see or hear her when I first came through the door.

I could also sense a gathering storm from the opposite end of a crowded room.

During family gatherings, I cringed whenever certain subjects came up, or someone said or did something.

To avoid trouble, I kept a running inventory of things that made my mother angry or upset. Anything with the potential for drama drove me to jump right up and try to fix it.

I was on my way to becoming an enabler. Nothing was more important to me than keeping my mother happy.

Mom never directly told anyone what she wanted. She threw out hints and expected people to get the message and comply.

She had a script of things she expected to be said and done at every family event. She never admitted to having an agenda, but if anyone missed a hint or clue, Mom became frustrated, angry, or, worst of all, burst into tears.

Years later, after she was diagnosed with cancer and required surgery, the doctor gave her Valium. It was the only medication she tried that lowered her high blood pressure.

That confirmed to me what I was not willing to admit. My mother may have suffered from some form of mental illness.

Her obsession with perfection didn't allow her to seek help. She could not admit to the emotional pain she suffered, the result of growing up in an unstable, alcoholic home.

Despite her strong faith and deep love of God, she did not have the strength to seek healing for herself.

Mom Knew Jesus Well: Perhaps I should have told you sooner, my mother was a reborn child of God. Perhaps what I have shared so far has led you to believe she was an ungodly woman.

She was in pain, but she loved Jesus with all her heart.

My mother met the Lord when she was very young. She said it happened during one of her parents' arguments.

She was hiding while they fought. Jesus came to comfort her.

Her death left a gaping hole in our lives. She loved many people and was loved by many people in return.

Mom's memorial service was packed. A steady stream of people came to the microphone to testify about her impact on their lives. Many mentioned how her smile reflected her love for God. She had a beautiful smile.

Daddy's Girl: My father is my hero. I will always be "Daddy's girl." His love and affirmation gave me the confidence to reach for my dreams.

Pain has sometimes cast a shadow over the foundation he gave me, but it has never shaken it.

Dad brought his pain into our family. Like my mother, he grew up trying to keep his mother happy. That carried over into his marriage. He worked hard to keep his wife happy, too.

Dad and I shared the same goal. Whatever it took to keep the peace, we did it. We twisted ourselves into whatever shape was necessary to please others, especially Mom.

Dad modeled the behavior, and I followed, believing it to be normal.

I have a brother who is nearly eight years younger than I. I will not try to tell you his story. It is his to tell.

Ch-Ch-Ch-Ch-Changes

I can best describe the past four decades of my life by noting some of the key moments that changed me.

Some were damaging and traumatic events. Others were times God spoke a healing revelation of truth to my heart.

Trauma: I define trauma as an emotionally-damaging event. It may be severe enough to leave physical as well as emotional scars. Trauma's signs may be invisible to others or evident to everyone.

An accident, a disease, or a natural disaster can lead to trauma. It can be the result of someone else's decisions and actions. It may also be self-inflicted.

Whatever the cause, trauma is often the result of something beyond our control. When there is nothing we can do to avoid being hurt, we feel powerless.

After trauma wounds us, we begin to act out of our pain and powerlessness. We may make choices an emotionally healthy person would never make.

We hurt ourselves, our loved ones, and people we don't even know. We feel powerless to do anything else.

Jesus Loves Me, This I Know: The first revelation to set the course of my life is when I knew, really knew, Jesus loved me.

He died for me. I didn't need to try to earn or deserve His love, nor was there anything I could do to lose it. He loved me!

The Christian Formation Center in Andover, Massachusetts, used to host a weekly charismatic Catholic mass and prayer meeting back in the seventies. The place was always packed.

More than five hundred people turned up every Thursday night, expecting the Spirit of God to move.[36]

On June 10th, 1976, my parents brought me there. It was an amazing and transformative night.

I had been trying hard to follow all the rules religion had laid out for me. I was trying to get God to show up and talk to me.

Nothing I tried worked. I remained disappointed.

That night, I met people filled with overflowing love, joy, and peace. I experienced the gentle, glorious power of God.

I knew Jesus loved me, not because I was a "good girl," but just because He did. I caught a glimpse of a love like that of my father, only higher - a constant and unchanging love.

My parents and I eagerly participated in the charismatic movement. God moved powerfully in those heady days. He used my parents in miraculous ways, yet at home, they were still hurting.

They were still carrying the damage done in their childhood.

Their pain was passed along to my brother and me.

Lord of My Life: I came to know I needed Jesus to be the Lord of my life. I wish I could tell you I fully understood what this meant when I was fifteen, but I did not. I only had an inkling.

It is a truth I continue to learn. Back then, I thought "making Jesus Lord" and "living by the Spirit" was like being on autopilot.

---

[36] Yes, we later used the same name for our ministry.

I thought if I could just "stay surrendered," I wouldn't do anything wrong or ever have any problems. I was wrong about that.

Acknowledging Jesus as the Lord of my life did not take away my freedom of choice. It also did not mean I would no longer make bad choices.

It certainly did not mean others would be unable to hurt me with their pain or choices.

Growing up in a home where my role was to rescue my mother and where my Mom and Dad's roles were to rescue everyone, it was only logical I would also seek out others to rescue.

No matter what I heard from the pulpit or read in books, I was determined to use dating as an "evangelism tool."

I thought if I loved a guy enough and could get him to love me, he would come to love Jesus.

If you have tried this, you know it doesn't work. I have yet to meet anyone who made it work. It's a lie.

Instead, they compromise their convictions and take a detour on their journey to wholeness

Toxic Relationships

Three relationships with men (boys, really) left me devastated.

The first one ended in date rape. I invested four years in the second one, trying to love an alcoholic and drug addict clean and sober.

It didn't work. I was always the designated sober person in our crowd. I continued to try to rescue him from the consequences of his drinking and using. I kept trying to please him to keep him from becoming angry.

I was always trying to become what he said he wanted me to be, only to anger and disappoint him when I failed. I lost myself.

Today that relationship would be considered abusive. I made it very easy for him to hurt me.

Was he wrong to say and do the hurtful things he did to me?

Yes! Absolutely!

But to be fair, I never told him he was hurting me when he hurt me.

I am not adopting or advocating a victim attitude that says, "Oh, he didn't mean it." or, "It was my fault. I made him do it."

I am telling you this out of my healing and empowerment.

Today I own the role I played in that relationship. If I had been emotionally healthy, I would never have tolerated or excused abusive behavior. I would never have started or stayed in the relationship.

I used the third relationship to get out of the second one. I didn't have enough strength to end it on my own. We both understood we were using one another. We even said so!

This relationship might not even be worth mentioning, except it brought me to the lowest point of despair in my life.

I did something that violated everything I believed.

I had an abortion.

I didn't realize how far I had walked away from God until I found myself lying on the clinic's bathroom floor afterward.

I cried out:

"Lord, I know you don't want me now, but I need you now."

Jesus answered. Not audibly, but very clearly:

"I'm glad we are talking again. You are going to be okay. I love you."

He was right, of course. I was going to be okay, but it took a long time to get there. It largely depends on what you consider "okay."

A Union of Equals

Soon after, Dad introduced me to Richard. We were perfectly suited to one another. We shared an equal passion for following Jesus.

We were also well matched in our pain, a recovering alcoholic and addict, and a recovering enabler. We were great partners and great mirrors for one another.

God has used us in each other's lives to reveal where we needed healing, where we needed to change our thinking, and where we needed to grow up.

Marriage has taught me to tell the truth. I know how to tell Richard how I feel and how to say so when I think he is wrong.

I have learned to believe him when he tells me I am intelligent, beautiful, or right about something on which we didn't initially agree.

I have also learned I don't have to jump up and try to "fix it" when my husband is grumpy and having a bad day.

My happiness is not dependent on him, but the Lord. Richard is okay with that. He feels the same way about his happiness.

When Eagles Cannot Fly

In the spring of 1995, a friend and I were visiting the zoo. We came to where the eagles lived. There were two of them. Their enclosure consisted only of a fence and a concrete moat.

There was no roof. It wasn't needed.

The eagles were flightless. Each had lost a wing to a poacher.

The sight of these magnificent creatures, meant to soar but bound for life to the earth, broke my heart.

My father teaches that Christians are like eagles. When they fly, eagles do not continually beat their wings the way most other birds do. They stretch them out and catch the wind.

Christians are supposed to soar by the power of the Holy Spirit, but instead of catching the wind with the wings God gave us, we flap them in a futile effort to make ourselves fly.

I was heartsick looking at those eagles because I felt like one of them. I had been walking out my faith and relationship with Jesus for twenty years, yet I still wasn't soaring. I still struggled.

The pain in my heart sometimes erupted in anger, in the same unpredictable way my mother's anger did. I still held back from telling people how I felt and what I thought.

I was still a people pleaser and an enabler.

None of these flaws was a blessing to my family. At that time, we were preparing to launch into full-time, living-on-the-road ministry.

We would be living in a fishbowl, on display for all to see. I did not see how I could ever measure up.

The eagles' caretaker was standing nearby, very excited. She pointed out the nest the pair had made on the ground.

The female eagle was sitting on a clutch of eggs. Eagles normally do not reproduce in captivity.

My heart broke some more.

Fall, then Fly: The most memorable of my father's eagle stories is his description of how baby eagles learn to fly.

Eagles build large nests in high places, on the edge of a cliff or in a tall, exposed tree. They make them with branches, twigs, and other things rough to the touch. Then they line the nest with soft material. The nest is ready now for the eggs.

When it is time for the babies to fly, their parents remove the nest's soft lining, making the babies uncomfortable.

When a baby eagle moves to the edge of the nest looking for a comfortable spot to sit, one of its parents pushes it out. The baby plummets toward the ground until it is scooped up at the last moment by their mother or father.

The adult eagle returns the fledgling to the nest. They do this again and again, until the young eagle opens its wings, grabs the wind, and soars just like its parents.

As I leaned against the railing watching the mother eagle proudly sitting on her eggs, a question reverberated in my soul:

"Can a flightless eagle teach her babies to fly?"

An uncomfortable question. I knew God was asking it. I had learned not to answer the Lord too quickly, but to think about it first whenever He asked questions like this one.

A few weeks later, Richard and I packed our two kids, four guitars, a sound system, a box of tapes, two tents, four sleeping bags, air mattresses, pillows, a food cooler, and our clothes into and on top of our two-door Ford Escort and hit the road.

That first trip, we traveled 7,000 miles in six weeks. We stayed in homes, a cabin, and at our favorite campground in Vermont.

I remember taking a nap on a two-hundred-year-old pew when it was the only hospitality given to us. We ministered together in churches. I stayed with the kids while Richard ministered in prisons.

It was wonderful. I knew we had stepped into our calling and begun to fulfill our purpose in life, but after six weeks, I was tired.

I was still worried I wasn't good enough. I didn't see how I could live up to expectations. I also worried about the effect our new nomadic lifestyle would have on our children. Above all, I wanted our kids to grow up whole. I wanted them to avoid the "preacher's kid syndrome" that plagues too many ministry kids.

Sitting by my favorite lake in Vermont, the question I had been avoiding for weeks came again:

"Can a flightless eagle teach her babies to fly?"

"No, Lord," I answered. "A flightless mother cannot teach her babies to fly."

With a higher intensity than the original question, the Lord's answer reverberated in my inner being:

"Then, let me heal you."

Beginning to Heal

My healing didn't happen all at once. It was a process, a series of moments, and lessons.

Healing came through prayer and contemplation. It came in conversation, in worship, and simple, day-to-day living.

The revelation truth I received from God was always on target, precisely what I needed.

The healing truth you need to hear from God will also be on target, meant just for you.

When it comes to our need for healing, one size does not fit all.

The Proactive Power of Choice

Possessing the power of choice means I am free to enjoy my friendship with God, and to be the person He created me to be.

I have learned I am the only one responsible for my actions, my emotions, my happiness, and my relationship with God and other people.

That's not to say the choices my husband and others close to me make, or things that happen to them don't affect me. They do, of course.

Things that happen to the most important people in my life can change my day, my week, and my life. The choices they make, for good or ill, can ripple like a rock thrown into a pond and affect my plans and my heart.

Becoming powerful and free means I have stopped trying to control things I cannot change. It also means I am the only one who can determine how I respond to circumstances beyond my control, such as other people's choices.

Enablers tend to react to others' choices rather than act on their initiative. Enablers program themselves to rescue others reflexively.

We come to believe we are powerless to do anything else. That is a lie. It only becomes true when we give in and make it true.

If I forget, God reminds me I am not powerless. He's given me the power to decide how to respond to other people's choices.

I even have the power not to respond at all!

I still occasionally act upon my first impulse, but because my decisions are conscious and deliberate rather than knee-jerk reactions, I no longer feel powerless.

Today I can decide whether to help someone and what the nature of that help will be. I choose when to speak and when to be silent. I consider whether my assistance will be beneficial or whether it will interfere with someone else's healing process.

I've found my decisions work best when I remember the second healing revelation of my life: Jesus is the Lord of my life.

When I ask Him what to do and how to follow through, I can trust Him to lead me to do what is right and best.

That doesn't mean I always see hoped-for results. People who ask for my input may choose to do something other than I suggest.

I also may not always hear what God is saying. No one on earth hears Him perfectly. But I have peace, knowing my choices today are mostly good ones.

Surrender Doesn't Always Mean, "I Give Up!"

Surrendering to the lordship of Jesus is not a one-time passive choice, but an ongoing exercise of the will.

We do not give up our power of choice when we surrender. If anything, living a life surrendered to Christ, empowers us! As we become more like Him, we get better at making the right decisions.

He also gives us more opportunities to make more choices!

If we are willing, He will lead us to each truth, each healing, each stage of growth we need. He wants us to become who we were born to be. He wants us to fulfill our destiny.

Growing in an intimate friendship of love and surrender with God is what the *My Recovery Community's* fifth and sixth core principles produce.

He enlivens our spirits, restores our minds, and heals our souls.

As we approach freedom, we begin to develop and manifest mature spiritual fruit.

How do you measure this kind of healing?

As I sit here at my daughter's kitchen table writing while I babysit my beautiful grandchildren,

I'd love to introduce you to the incredible freedom that comes from actively pursuing your healing.

Mother's Day

Let me tell you one more story that demonstrates the extent of my healing.

In June of 2004, my mother learned she had cancer. She died on Easter Sunday in 2005.

Her final months may have been the most difficult but also the most amazing, joyful season of my life.

Never have I experienced so much heartache and seen so much healing at the same time.

During this season of impending loss, I often marveled at who I had become through the healing power of God. I was no longer a people-pleasing chameleon. I had come to be myself, my real self, as God had intended me to be.

I was strong, even though my mother had always implied women were not strong. I was honest, though I learned at a young age to tell my mother only what she wanted to hear.

I was intelligent, despite a childhood spent hiding my active mind to avoid upsetting Mom.

I was me! The love I felt for my mother was right and real, rather than a distortion pressed through a disfiguring mold. In her final months, I was able to give her the gift of the real me.

Even more surprising, not only did my mother like and accepted the real me, but she also came to depend on those traits of my true nature she had rejected in the past.

Mom and I found healing and joy at her bedside. I watched as Jesus healed the wounds of her childhood.

I remember one night thanking Father and asking Him:

"Can I keep her? She would be so much more fun now that you've healed her."

He told me no. My mother had finished her race. Father God knew she had learned all she needed to know in this life. She was ready to move on into eternity.

Though my mother's pain caused me much pain, I do not remember her that way. I can acknowledge the reality of my past when asked to share it, but my healing is complete.

Past traumas no longer darken my life.

Today I remember how much my mother loved me and delighted in her family. I remember how her face lit up when our extended "spiritual family" gathered around her dining room table for food and fellowship.

I remember how she poured her love and affection into my children and made holidays memorable, especially Easter and Christmas.

Our family tells stories about her. We laugh when something reminds us of her, or when one of us says something she would have said.

We give ourselves "Tootsie points" when we do something that would have made her happy.[37]

We buy Marshmallow Peeps because she bought them. We laugh because, since her death, Peeps are on our table for every holiday when before she died, they only appeared at Easter. We are sure she is responsible.

My mother is part of me. Not because she hurt me, but despite the hurt. She also left me a legacy of joy.

---

[37] Her grandchildren called her "Grandma Tootsie.".

273

No one recovers alone. God can use one family member's healing to reach and heal the rest of the family.

Despite past pain and present challenges, every member of my immediate family has sought and continues to enjoy everything Jesus has given us.

He has given us healing, purpose, and freedom.

Today I watch my family fly. I watch my daughter teach her children to fly. I sit in wonder as other people learn to fly through the loving ministry of our volunteers and chaplains.

God's love for me is more profound and more robust than I know. He is still working out the good He has for me.

He still seeks out and gently touches the hidden places of past pain, things I have forgotten, and the occasional new pain that comes from living in our wounded world.

Life with Christ is a journey, an incredible, beautiful journey.

Even when life is hard.

May your journey bring you joy and peace.

May your life be fruitful.

May you live the life you were born to live.

A QUICK REVIEW

This book has the potential to relieve the suffering of only God knows how many people trapped in the vicious downward spiral of addictive behavior. There is a lot in it to absorb.

For that reason, we want to be sure the most critical points in this book are not buried in the details surrounding them. So, let us summarize them:

The Key Points

❖ Addictive behavior takes many forms. It does not always involve the use or abuse of drugs or alcohol.

❖ Twelve-step recovery only works for 5-10% of those who seek help. It does not address the emotional root cause of addiction.

❖ If traditional recovery programs work for you, keep going. We just need something else for the majority for whom it does not work.

❖ The emotional root cause of addictive behavior is a sense or spirit of powerlessness.

❖ The antidote for powerlessness and the addictive behavior it produces is not admitting we are powerless over our addiction; the remedy is empowerment to beat it!

❖ The loss of the power to make our own choices creates pervasive, unhealthy anger, and opens the door for other potentially harmful emotions.

❖ God did not intend humans to experience emotional pain. That is why we are not very good at dealing with it.

❖ We use for three reasons: to numb or avoid our pain, to regain a sense of having power, or to recapture a lost "first love" feeling.

❖ The <u>decision</u> to use, not the use itself, makes us feel "better." The decision to use restores our sense of having power.

❖ No one likes being told what to do. That is why telling someone they <u>must</u> do something is counter-productive— - most people will push-back.

❖ To get buy-in instead of push-back, we don't tell people what to do.

❖ How each of us recovers is not up to any program, mentor, or any other person, to decide. How we recover is entirely up to us. If we decide to do it, we own it!

❖ Recovery is good. It is just not complete.

❖ Freedom is complete. When we talk about freedom, we are talking about freedom in Christ.

❖ It is possible to recover without a higher power, but freedom in Christ is not possible without Christ.

❖ Jesus offers us everything we need to be free. He is the way, the truth, and the life.

THE MY RECOVERY COMMUNITY

My Recovery is an online community offering a variety of regularly scheduled weekly meetings. Addicts and those who love them can attend using a smartphone or computer.

For information and directions on how to attend a meeting, visit noonerecoversalone.org and click on the My Recovery Online photo.

You are a member if you say you are. You are free to come and go at will.

You may remain anonymous or use your real name. It's your choice.

Our purpose is:

- ❖ To empower addicts and family members alike to defeat the spirit of powerlessness that may be holding us back.

- ❖ To take back and exercise our God-given power of choice.

- ❖ To stop our addictive behavior once and for all.

- ❖ To facilitate the healing of painful memories and emotions that lead us to self-medicate.

- ❖ To help us live the full, free life we were born to live.

The Six Core Principles of the My Recovery Community

1. You are not powerless! Only you have the power to decide what to do.

2. We will not tell you what to do. Instead, we ask, "What do you want to do?"

3. No one recovers alone. Recovery works best when addicts, family members, friends, and the community recover together.

4. Relapse doesn't mean we start over. The time we remained clean and sober still counts. Relapse reveals where we still need healing.

5. Permanent freedom from addiction is not only possible; it is God's desire. God works in us to bring about spiritual rebirth, cognitive regeneration, the healing restoration of our souls, and the development of mature spiritual fruit.

6. True, lasting freedom begins when we accept Jesus' offer of friendship. We become the person we were born to be. We live the life we were born to live.

A BENEDICTION

Two of the fundamental needs every human being has is to know who we are and why we are here. We find our answers as we get to know Jesus as Savior, Friend, and Older Brother.

Anything less than this ideal causes us pain.

Pain leads us to settle for substitutes that may provide relief for a season, but in the end, only add to our suffering.

If you are angry at God or unable to believe He exists, we are not going to twist your arm to persuade you otherwise.

He is perfectly able to make Himself known to you. He is willing and able to make you whole.

We will not tell you what to do. Only you have the right and the power to decide what to do with your life.

Revelation 3:20 "Behold, I stand at the door and knock; if anyone hears My voice and opens the door, I will come in to him and will dine with him, and he with Me."

Not even God will make your decisions for you. He waits at the door of your heart for you to invite Him in.

He will not knock your door down and invade your space.
Love doesn't use force.

So, here we are at last. Our final encouragement to you:

May you decide to get free and stay free. May you live the life you were born to live, instead of settling for crumbs from life's table.

May God bless you and keep you safe on your journey to wholeness.

May your journey be fruitful.

May you pass through times of testing and come out on the other side stronger than before you went in.

May you become powerful. May you become free.

We hope to see you in *My Recovery Community*.

ABOUT THE AUTHORS

Bishop Richard H. and Reverend Dawn Marie Johnson have been engaged in full-time ministry throughout the United States and Canada since 1994.

For almost ten of those years, Richard, Dawn, and their kids lived full-time in a fifth-wheel trailer in church parking lots all over North America.

They had ministered in thirty-eight states and four Canadian provinces by the time they came off the road in 2005. They led thousands of people to the Lord. They brought comfort and encouragement to hurting people in prisons, jails, juvenile detention centers, residential re-entry programs, churches, home fellowships, and many other venues.

In January of 2005, Richard and Dawn started *Christian Formation Ministries, Inc. (CFM)* in New Albany, Indiana. Their volunteers and Community Chaplains minister to inmates, addicts, their children, and their immediate families, both inside and outside prison.

Married in 1985, Richard and Dawn have two grown children; Rev. Suzanna Jacobson and Jimmy Johnson, and three (so far) grandchildren.

Suzanna took over the leadership of CFM in 2015. She is a gifted leader and motivator.

Jimmy quietly ministers to young people involved in the online international gaming community. He manages a tabletop gaming store in Lousiville, Kentucky.

Bishop Richard is a teacher, trainer, and musicianary, a purveyor of "Christian swamp music," with numerous recordings to his credit.

He was known for years as "Stonefingers" except in Arkansas, where they just called him "Stone."

Richard was ordained a Minister of the Gospel in 1995 and commissioned a Bishop and Apostle in 2017.

He did such an excellent job during his years as a Prison Chaplain that they shut down the facility where he served.[38]

Richard is involved in the *My Recovery Community* and other aspects of CFM's ministry; He also mentors church and parachurch ministry leaders. He continues to write books, music, life skills curricula, ministry training materials, resources for recovery and reentry, and scripture commentaries.

Reverend Dawn is a fifth-generation minister and a gifted teacher, preacher, and exhorter. You might say it's in her blood.

She was ordained a Minister of the Gospel in 2000.

Dawn is a wife, mother, grandmother, and the co-founder of Christian Formation Ministries.

She has also enjoyed success in the business world as a trainer, curriculum writer, and IT specialist. Her business-related skills are extremely useful in ministry.

---

[38] Not really; he just likes to say that. But they did close the prison.

She is CFM's Volunteer and Chaplaincy Training Director and develops many of our unique ministry resources.

An experienced prison minister and mentor, Dawn has tremendous discernment and is gifted by God to facilitate the healing of past emotional traumas and the pain they cause.

Inviting Richard and Dawn to Minister

Richard and Dawn are available, individually or together, to minister anywhere in the United States and Canada.

They are also available to minister outside North America on request.

For scheduling information, please contact:

Kerith Resources
PO Box 432
Jeffersonville, Indiana, USA 47131-0432
Richard@christian-formation.org

For information about Christian Formation Ministries
and the My Recovery Community,
please visit noonerecoversalone.org.

Made in the USA
Monee, IL
04 November 2021